Disrupting Time

Aaron Stark

© 2022

New York

Cover Art:
- Jacques David (right, public domain)
- Theo Gribi (left, public domain)
- Main Building, Centennial Exhibition (public domain)
- 1903 Waltham Watch dial (author's photo)

Back cover:
- Inside the Main Building, Centennial Exhibition (public domain)
- 1903 Waltham Watch (author's photo)

Table of Contents

Prologue

Disruption: "(1) to break apart; to throw into disorder. (2) to interrupt the normal course or unity of"

- Merriam-Webster Dictionary[1]

The old factory of the American Watch Company of Waltham, Massachusetts, sits like a retired warship on the banks of the Charles River outside Boston, a reminder of long-forgotten industrial combat. Once the site of one of the nation's great industrial enterprises, it now blends into the background of other dilapidated industrial-era districts across the country.

In the second half of the nineteenth century, the Waltham Watch Company, as it became known, transformed the entire global watch market by bringing modern production, marketing, and sales techniques to an otherwise artisanal industry. A labor reformer and former editor of the New York Times, upon touring the factory in 1887 wrote: "I found myself before one of the most remarkable industrial establishments ever built; the largest watch factory in the world, the oldest in the United States, the most perfect in every way, yet devised by human genius — the American Waltham Watch factory." The writer continued to describe an ambiance that made the impressive factory an inviting workplace: "It is a vast series of buildings presenting a frontage of nearly eight hundred feet, and with wings, towers, courts and offices. In front of it is the umbrageous park and behind it the gleaming river."[2]

In 1870, a popular magazine of the era noted the presumed staying power and future value of Waltham. It foretold that in a hundred years:

> A white-haired man shall say: "My son, when I pass away I shall leave you this watch. It has been in our family for a century: it was made at the great centre of the watch manufacture Waltham, and was one of their earliest productions, when they had revolutionized the industry and transplanted it to the New World..."[3]

Ironically, this sentiment is similar to the modern marketing pitch of one of the most resilient and famous Swiss watch companies, Patek Philippe, a renowned watchmaker in 1870 and which remains a sought-after brand today. Its slogan advertises: "you never really own a Patek Philippe, you merely look after it for the next generation." Unlike Patek Philippe, the prestige Waltham enjoyed in 1870 has not survived into the modern era. An overwhelming number of Americans have never heard of the Waltham Watch Company, even among the residents of its namesake city.

In contrast, Waltham's Swiss watchmaking competitors are still thriving, with many now situated in high-tech buildings in the mountainous region of western Switzerland. Swiss companies use the latest machinery to continue to manufacture mechanical watches. They have luxury boutiques in malls across the world. A luxury watch made by Patek Philippe, Vacheron Constantin, and Audemars Piguet, among others, can even be purchased for tens of thousands of dollars in the upscale boutiques of downtown Boston a short ten miles from the site of the now-defunct

Waltham Watch Company. Each of those listed was one of Waltham's 1876 competitors.

This book addresses some of the origins of that paradox through the perspectives of Waltham and the Swiss. It specifically examines the years 1857 to 1900. This period catalyzed modern, industrial watch production and solidified the Swiss' role as the world's best watchmakers, a reputation which has endured through many subsequent chapters of their history.

Discovering the story

I have always been interested in the history of watches and became intrigued by the all-but-abandoned Waltham factory outside Boston, near where I was attending Harvard Business School. I had heard about Waltham having inherited a 1903 watch from my great-grandfather. I began reading anything I could about Waltham. I soon came across the English translation of a report written by the Swiss watchmaker and engineer Jacques David following his visit to the United States in 1876.[4]

He specifically directed much of his attention toward Waltham. David attended the Centennial Exhibition, the same place where Waltham would win awards for producing the best luxury watches in the world and where David had seen the Waltham Watch Company's lauded assembly line exhibit in operation. Following his three-month visit, David wrote a report describing the American watch industry. The report documented American watchmaking procedures, factory operations, financial conditions, and operations management.

He recorded more than I had ever known about the American watch industry and described a factory narrative that countered my understanding of the industrial revolution. It was a unique account of the exceptional treatment of workers in the industrial era, a time when income inequality approached its peak in the Gilded Age, and the mistreatment of workers became a national issue. The report was written only six months before the Great Strike of 1877, a riot by railroad employees across the country that ultimately left twenty people killed by the state militia.[5]

Given the level of detail in David's report, I found it curious that the well-published historian David Landes had told of the Swiss recovery in his landmark book *Revolution in Time* (1983) with no mention of David or his report. Landes' book is the most often referenced history of the watch industry. As it turned out, David's report was mainly kept secret at the time of his writing and was not widely available to the public until 1992.[6]

After its 1992 public release, David's name began to appear in written accounts about the watch industry, including mentions by leading scholars such as Pierre-Yves Donze and appearing in the reference notes of Alexis McCrossen.[7] Both historians' books are the most recent major works about timekeeping and horology history. Donze's book is even titled *History of the Swiss Watch Industry from Jacques David to Nicholas Hayek* (2015). But why had it taken so long for David to be recognized and his report to be published?

Putting the pieces together

I began to research the history of David's report and its connection to the Centennial Exhibition. The

8

previous and conventional narrative was that American companies, notably Waltham, freely and naively shared information about their novel systems with the Swiss, which David then documented in a report. But this conception was at odds with the evidence I found, which clearly showed that David was an industrial spy. I looked for further confirmation of my suspicions and came across a 1987 Swiss academic article that, in a brief mention, also called David a spy, where the author titled David an "En veritable espion industriel" ("real industrial spy").[8] It was apparent that there was more to the story than had made it into the conventional narrative and the common histories of the watch industry.

During my subsequent research, I discovered a fascinating tale of cutthroat competition, industrial espionage, societal development, and a great world's fair. The competition in this era was so intense it was even referred to as "combat of industry" by one contemporary observer.[9] The Swiss watchmakers and Waltham viewed their situation through such a lens, using similar bellicose imagery. David would refer to the American watch companies as "a courageous and well armed adversary."[10] Meanwhile, Waltham's chief executive also viewed the situation as a protracted war: "if we can't live in peace we must live on a war-footing...I propose to make the fighting as effective as possible."[11]

The role of the watch industry in society

The watch industry of 1876 occupied a different role in society than it does today. In preparing this book, one scholar observed that David's espionage occurred *because* the watchmaking industry was so central to the development of the late nineteenth century.[12] Historian Lewis Mumford wrote in his seminal work *Technics and Civilization* (1934): "the clock has been the foremost machine in modern technics: and at each period it has remained in the lead...The clock, moreover, served as a model for many other kinds of mechanical works."[13] Therefore, the watch industry of the nineteenth century (and the clock industry before it) was more akin to the modern technology sector than today's jewelry industry.

Watches were a central part of the market and a key to economic growth. Mumford observed: "The Clock, not the steam engine, is the key machine of the modern industrial age."[14] Everything from the societal consciousness of the hour to the timing of railroads to scientific management to the precision tool industry could trace their roots to the clock and watch industries.

The Swiss have a long history of watchmaking, with a few key eras that have defined what we know of the industry today. This book only addresses one of those critical chapters. It is a chronicle of strategy, competition, espionage, decisions, and consequences that shaped the global watch market at the turn of the twentieth century. It is the account of a remarkable turn of events driven by cunning spies, visionary leaders, and strategic choices that put the Swiss and American watch industries on entirely different trajectories. Had the events of 1876 never happened, we would likely know little about Swiss watches today.

The themes of this book are explored through the eyes of Waltham, the Swiss watchmakers, and their main characters: Royal Robbins, Ambrose Webster,

Jacque David, Theophilus Gribi, and Edouard Favre-Perret. This is the story of industrial combat, an industry 'broken apart' and 'thrown into disorder,' and how a cottage industry of Swiss watchmakers organized to defeat an American industrial power.

This is the story of *Disrupting Time*.

A note on sources:

This book primarily uses original sources, many of which were written over 100 years ago. I also use secondary sources to verify claims or to see how others have interpreted events. I found many secondary sources disagree about various topics, often for good reason. Sometimes information was unknown or unpublished for decades. Additionally, nineteenth century authors wrote in a style that we would equate to an opinion piece in the modern era. In many cases, primary sources are non-existent and secondary sources cite other secondary sources that do not trace back to a primary source.

When instances of conflicting information arose, I used the source which was most verifiable or plausible. Despite the care taken, this will undoubtedly result in disagreements over the interpretations of various passages. Additionally, there were individual cases where the primary source was wrong and more recent research provides a more accurate read. These cases were rare and are elaborated in the end notes.

Chapter 1:
In the Palace of Industry

Opening day of the 1876 Centennial Exhibition in Fairmount Park, Philadelphia (Centennial Photographic Company, Public Domain)

Centennial Exhibition – June 1876

    In the summer of 1876, Philadelphia's Centennial Exhibition celebrated America's first 100 years. The Exhibition represented the rapid advances of the world, but primarily America's industrial success and massive economic growth. While still a very young country by most standards, America was establishing itself on the global stage.

Alexander Graham Bell, the inventor of the telephone, which would debut at the Centennial, wrote about the Exhibition: "It is wonderful! You can have no idea of it till you see it. It grows upon one. It is so prodigious and so wonderful that it absolutely staggers one to realize what the word 'Centennial Exhibition' means. Just think of having the products of all nations condensed into a few acres of buildings."[15]

Almost 10 million people would visit the Centennial across its six months of operation. Walking through the grounds and buildings, one joined the sea of humanity assembled from all over the world. [16] It was described as a "journey around the world, giving an insight into the life and thought of all manner of men, and lifting the visitor above the narrow limits of his surroundings, so that his horizon stretched out to embrace the whole human race. Bigotry, conceit, and local pride vanished as the great panorama of the achievements of mankind, of all races and in all climes, passed before his eyes."[17]

The Centennial Exhibition displayed national progress, but the descriptions of visitors emphasized the clash of attitudes in America at a time that promoted nationalistic feelings and protectionism. It was not apparent that Americans were ready for the assortment of people who attended from all over the world. The same author of the previous passage also noted the "stalwart Indian that stalks through the hall…the small but alert Japanese…the 'Heathen Chinee' with his almond-eyes and long pig-tails, his comical dress, and his 'ways that are dark and tricks that are vain,' [and] the turbaned Turk."[18]

At the epicenter of the Centennial's 2,470 acreages lay the Main Building and Machinery Hall, which enclosed the central plaza that welcomed visitors to the world's fair. The Main Building was impressive, being the largest enclosed space in the world at the time.[19]

Inside the Main Building, fountains fired gushes of water, and music occasionally filled the air. Sometimes the Centennial's organ broke through the cacophony of exhibitors and visitors. Everyone was universally amazed: "On all sides were heard exclamations of wonder and delight. Few had imagined the Exhibition either so extensive or so grand an affair, and all were delighted."[20] Endless showcases, country areas, national flags and banners, people from all over the world, the unceasing pandemonium, the musty stench of thousands of people crowding the hall, and the severe heat that soaked the glass-covered building in the summer sun.[21]

Across the plaza from the Main Building was Machinery Hall, a much smaller but equally impressive building housing much of the emerging technology of the era. To those visiting the Centennial, Machinery Hall was a temple of innovation and a palace of industry. The machines shown in the hall were symbolic of the advancement made by humankind over the previous decade. During the opening ceremonies, the visitors to the Centennial even bowed their heads in prayer to thank God for America's "social and national prosperity and progress, for valuable discoveries and multiplied inventions, for labor-saving machinery relieving the toiling masses."[22]

The Hall was constructed with glass, iron, and wood, standing 70 feet tall and extending over a quarter mile. At the center of the palace of industry was the 800-ton Corliss Steam Engine that rose 45 feet tall. It symbolized the industrial horsepower that America provided to the burgeoning global economy. The two 44-inch cylinders served as the ventricles of this mechanical heart, producing 1,400 horsepower that supplied the lifeblood to the machines in the entire Hall through a two-mile-long venous network of shafts and belts. One visitor described the Corliss engine as "a sight to behold – a sight for a lifetime."[23]

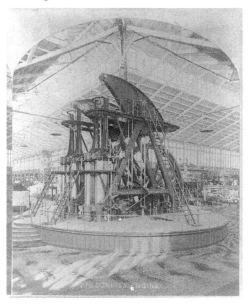

Corliss Engine circa 1876 (Public Domain)

"The One that Cuts the Screws"

Despite showcasing many physically large inventions, those with the most poignant effect in the years following were ones with more delicate intricacies and had a much smaller presence at the Centennial.

Alexander Graham Bell's first telephone debuted in the Main Building and could be experienced on each end of the hall.

The German area displayed novel machines powered by "a series of explosions" where "gas and air are mixed in such proportions as to give an explosive compound," demonstrating early examples of the combustion engine.[24] In addition, the Centennial featured the monorail that could be ridden across the grounds. It also showcased the sewing machine and typewriter.

Theophilus Gribi, shown later in life. From "Horology," June 1937 (Public Domain).

Theophilus Gribi was one of the visitors who would leave the Centennial having had his entire imagination altered as the fair revealed the frighteningly novel advances made by American inventors. Gribi was a middle-aged Swiss man. He had arrived from Switzerland into Philadelphia in the spring of 1876. The watchmakers of the mountainous regions of Switzerland sent him to the Centennial Exhibition to serve as a judge at the world's fair while searching for reasons why Swiss watch sales had declined by almost 80% from 1872 to 1876, a sharp decrease for Switzerland's primary market.[25] Gribi was a skilled watchmaker and had spent much of his career working in Philadelphia for the jeweler Bailey, Banks, and Biddle, only recently moving back to his native Switzerland.[26] He was an ideal choice for this seemingly innocuous mission of discovery.

Gribi arrived before the opening celebrations on May 10th. There was one company that Gribi noticed that was almost certainly set up on time and operating on the opening day. This American company was organized and calculated, showing something so novel that Gribi struggled to describe the ingenuity. His concern was a machine displayed by the Waltham Watch Company, about the size of a large shoebox, operated by a young woman.

The disturbing machine was Waltham's proprietary automatic screw-making machine. The nickel-plated machine with robot-like arms could produce a tiny screw every five seconds. This was a rate so fast it was not even worth calculating the efficiency compared to that of a skilled watchmaker in Switzerland, though Gribi felt compelled to try. He took out his notepad and scribbled a note: "Screw machine

18

make[s] 17 screws a minute 10,200[27] per day."[28] This figure was significant because it was at least eight to ten times more efficient than anyone Gribi knew.

This machine captured the imagination of correspondents and tourists alike. A San Francisco newspaper wrote: "It would be impossible to describe in detail the many operations of ingenious machines one can see in the making of these watches in Machinery Hall. [Waltham's] space is surrounded from morning till night to see the delicate and yet swift workings of the machines, particularly that which cuts the screws."[29]

The device automatically fed a small piece of wire and then began to form the screw from the wire, which was then cut. A tiny mechanical pincer reached over, grabbed the screw, slotted the head, finished it, and dropped it into a small bin for collection. All in five seconds. Even more shocking was that one person could operate ten machines simultaneously. This system multiplied the potential output of a single worker from 1,000 to 80,000 screws in a single day. The screw machine worked so effectively that it would remain in use at Waltham until its final closure in 1954 and even longer at another company until 1981.[30]

The automatic screw-making machine was not the only noteworthy aspect of Waltham's exhibit. Visitors also noticed the overwhelming presence of Waltham's women employees, thirteen of the eighteen total workers at the exhibit.[31] Women's participation in the labor force was something of a debut at the Exhibition, which, in addition to the machinery, the women were also blessed during the opening prayer: "We pray thy benediction especially on the women of America, who for the first time in the history of our race take so conspicuous a place in our national celebration."[32]

One writer visiting the Exhibition noted the presence of the women working the Waltham exhibit as if they were meant to be decorative flourishes. While the writer only chose to comment on three exhibits from Machinery Hall, he noted that Waltham "has its machinery and its pretty girls at work, making every part of a watch, and keeping jealous wives on the watch, as their husbands suddenly become interested in the wonderful mechanical manipulation of that delicate machinery and those deft fingers. This alone is worth going a hundred miles to see."[33]

The capabilities and appearance of the Waltham exhibit were no accident. While Machinery Hall was a temple devoted to mechanical ingenuity, for Waltham it was an opportunity to show the world the superiority of its pocket watches and production methods. It allowed the company to demonstrate to competitors that it could produce enough watches to dominate the global watch market through quality mass production. That was the goal of treasurer Royal E. Robbins, who served as Waltham's chief executive and principal owner.

Some viewed displaying Waltham's proprietary machines in operation at the Centennial as a risk. Competition in the American watch industry was fierce. The Centennial Exhibition offered Waltham a chance to demonstrate its superiority like an advancing army parading through the streets of captured watch markets. Robbins had convinced investors that there could be "no greater discouragement" to competitors "than by the free exhibition of the factory itself and of all it contains."[34] He was most concerned about the American competition, which had become numerous and taxing in the years leading up to the Centennial. Discouraging further American competition was his primary goal.

The large Corliss Engine in Machinery Hall. The Waltham exhibit sits just feet from it and can be seen to the bottom right of the Engine with 3 white windows (Centennial Photographic Company, Public Domain)

In the end, the company's shareholders were complicit in approving his plan to display and operate the machines in front of millions of visitors. Many investors did not believe this was wise, but the shareholders trusted Robbins.[35] He was a well-respected businessman who had served on the board of directors for companies like the Union Pacific Railroad (1871-1874), acting alongside Andrew Carnegie and George Pullman.[36] Additionally, Robbins' careful selection of machines ensured that not *everything* would be on display.

The Waltham exhibit was deliberately planned to demonstrate the production of a select few pieces or parts of the watch. The purpose was a calculated demonstration of Waltham's dominance over its American competitors and the irrelevance of the handmade Swiss watch.[37] Waltham was cautious to ensure its trade secrets would not be given away. It had no interest in the free sharing of ideas nor the promotion of competitors' advances.

The shock of Philadelphia

The exhibit served its purpose. What Gribi saw was enough to call into question the Swiss watch industry's future existence. By 1876, watchmaking was a national industry for Switzerland, a source of pride and an exhibition of Swiss skill. As Waltham's machines produced precision wheels, pinions, and screws for a mechanical watch, which were usually produced by an artisan in a home in Switzerland, one American newspaper gloated that old-world observers like Gribi, "gaze in astonishment [and] apparently admit that their occupation is going, if not gone."[38]

There was nothing the Swiss watchmakers could do that would match Waltham's automatic screw machines, not to mention the rest of the company's capabilities. After just a few days of observing the machines, Gribi wrote: "I have been examining, as an expert on the jury, the products and tools of the Waltham Watch Company (Massachusetts) and I must admit that I was filled with admiration for their watches of various types and quality, and for the splendid machines and tools that this factory has exhibited."[39] However, the problem was not isolated to Waltham's machines or its watches. The Swiss disadvantage lay in the industrial mindset for the Swiss did not have the American penchant for mass production innovation, which seemed to multiply yearly.

One member of Switzerland's delegation to the Centennial Exhibition, a shoemaker named Edward Bally, quickly and accurately recognized the dire position of the Swiss watch industry. He knew that machines and mass production were only symptoms of a more significant problem emanating from American ingenuity. "Have you ever compared a rake, a spade, a knife, a hatchet, made in America, with tools made here? How much Europe is left behind!" he wrote.[40]

Bally owned the largest shoe factory in Europe and had already experimented with copying American production methods. He had paid American engineers to install American-made machines in his shoe factory. Yet, even through imitation of American techniques, he could not compete with the Americans. Shoes produced in Massachusetts were brought to his European factory, having traveled the ocean for a fee, and then presented to him for a price below his cost of production.[41] He claimed that his employees "work also with American machines. They have the same tools, [yet] their productive capacity is far inferior to that of the American operative."[42] From Bally's point of view, attempting to imitate the Americans was not enough to match American industry or its workers.[43]

Bally noted that Americans had an inherent advantage over the Europeans that emerged from structures within the professional economy. Europeans learned a specialized craft over decades through apprenticeship and repeated exactly what their master taught them. In contrast, most Americans had no artisanal skills and had to invent production methods that substituted for their lack of skill. This led to unimaginable improvements in designs and production methods in many American industries.[44] Even if the Swiss could replicate the American machines and work ethic, there was little encouragement they could ever match American innovation.

This was industrial combat. According to Bally, America had "armed itself as for a battle for the moment when it would have to enter upon the peaceful combat of industry... The world has never seen so considerable a sum of new ideas and of applications of these new ideas as that which was presented by the Exhibition at Philadelphia."[45]

The growing technology sector of its era

Watches were the emerging technology of the era. They presented an opportunity for growth and immense wealth for whichever producer could gain a competitive advantage in the market. Watches and timekeepers were not as novel as the telephone but were far more relevant to the average person's needs.

The shift towards time consciousness had accelerated during the American Civil War, which had ended only eleven years prior. Soldiers had become dependent and somewhat addicted to time. Before the attack on Vicksburg, General Ulysses Grant emphasized the importance of timekeeping to his army by ordering that all watches be synchronized. Many soldiers worried they would not survive the impending attack. Before the battle, one Union soldier gave his watch to a friend, saying, "this watch I want you to send to my father if I never return," demonstrating the importance of timekeepers, not just for their utility but also for their connection with the owner.[46] Society for so many millennia had thrived on a generalized concept of time. With the synchronized maneuvers of warfare and the increasing distribution of watches, timekeeping was becoming central to society.

Following the Civil War, a population of time-driven soldiers from all ranks left the service, and society became indentured to punctuality. Watches were much more than jewelry; instead a critical tool that was quickly becoming a part of life. Public clocks still served as the primary source of time as they were universally accessible, though not ubiquitous in their location.[47] In contrast, the watch allowed people to harness time in their pockets if they could afford one. Historian Alexis McCrossen noted: "The pocket watch was an indispensable part of the self-made American's tool kit. It was a vehicle of self-realization, rather than a privilege and inheritance."[48]

Historian Michael O'Malley noted that beginning in 1870 and continuing into the twentieth century, advertisements pushed Americans to view mechanical timekeepers as essential. Among other things, the advertisements of the era promoted that "standardized clock time [was] a tool of education and industry, a sort of uniform that all laborers in the commercial army were required to put on at childhood and wear through life."[49] An 1870 journal article exemplified this: "ingenuity and perseverance have compassed the possibility of [the watch's] endless multiplication. Once the luxury of the rich only, it is now the necessity of all."[50]

Within four years after the Centennial, the societal transformation towards punctuality would be virtually complete. O'Malley noted that by 1880, "Americans experienced one aspect of this reformation of time consciousness in a new emphasis on strict punctuality in work, in private life and at public events, theaters and concerts."[51] Thus, the 1876 Centennial found itself amidst a revolution in timekeeping.

The price range of most watches, even 'affordable' watches, was still expensive for the era. The necessity and desire for watch ownership drove consumers to spend a notable portion of their annual income on a watch to be able to tell the time in a punctually driven economy.[52] In 1870, about one in every twenty-one American adults owned a watch, making ownership far from universal, but the increasing importance of timekeeping meant that demand was on the rise. Within thirty years, ownership would quadruple to an estimated one in every five American adults.[53]

As the societal shift began, the Swiss watchmakers responded to the growing demand. The Swiss were willing to produce any quality of watch; few of the watches sold were works of art. The average quality was so dubious that American publications of the era portrayed the Swiss as if they were equivalent to an untrustworthy but mass-producing emerging economy.

One publication wrote: "such is her unrivalled cheapness of production that she has undermined the manufacture in the other European countries, which now send to Switzerland to have the pieces of their own watches made."[54] The devolution into poor quality was aptly captured in an English publication of the era:

During the time of prosperity of the trade a good many [Swiss] agricultural labourers [left] their former occupation and dedicate[d] themselves to the watch industry. A superabundance of hands soon ensued, accompanied by a falling of wages, and besides, the quality of the products manufactured became yearly worse and worse. Only some few tradesmen continued to manufacture watches of higher qualities, while the majority of them supplied the markets with the lowest kind of products...An over confidence in monopoly led to deterioration of the article. The result was that Swiss watches fell into discredit in the United States.[55]

Even widely read publications such as *Appleton's Journal* began heralding the problem. *Appleton's* wrote that Swiss "products of a fraudulent commerce are scattered broadcast over the country, while its victims are taxed millions of dollars annually for the repair of shabby and dishonest work."[56] The Swiss leaders later acknowledged allowing their fellow citizens to take advantage of America's increasing demand, sending the "worst trash" to unsuspecting customers an ocean away.[57]

The panic of 1873

By some measures, watches were Switzerland's most important export industry, and America was the top consumer. One Swiss leader referred to America as Switzerland's "milk cow."[58] 1873 would prove to be a critical year for the Swiss industry, marking the beginning of the Panic of 1873, which would turn into a

27

global depression, the worst of which struck from 1873 to 1879. Exports of Swiss watches to America suddenly dropped from 366,000 in 1872 to 75,000 by 1876.[59] The Swiss were alarmed to see their U.S. exports fall, but the Panic provided a facade for an underlying shift in the watch industry that was taking place simultaneously.

SWISS EXPORTS TO UNITED STATES V. WALTHAM
PRODUCTION

(Author's work)

While the Swiss focused on the Panic of 1873 as a central cause of declining exports, Waltham was advancing and growing (see chart above). During this period, and leading up to it, Waltham was earning an untarnished reputation. The official history of the Centennial noted: "The Waltham watches have long been regarded as the best of American manufacture, and the universal testimony of all who have used them is that they are unexcelled by any in the world."[60] A prominent Swiss watchmaker, upon seeing Waltham's exhibit confessed: "I personally have doubted that competition. But now I have seen — I have felt it — and am terrified by the danger to which our industry is exposed."[61]

It had finally set in – it was not the Panic of 1873 that caused Switzerland's "milk cow" to run dry, but rather a quickly growing American industry that had unequivocally transformed the existing market order. David would observe: "Business [in America] is rock bottom as far as concerns Swiss watches. They do not want to see them, they do not want to talk about them and everyone is undercutting his neighbour to get rid of any stock he has, without success."[62] In June 1876, Gribi wrote to his fellow watchmakers in Switzerland: "we have been left behind."[63]

Jacques David

As news arrived back in Switzerland describing the watchmakers' situation at the Centennial Exhibition, the Swiss watchmakers' professional society decided to send an additional expert to join Gribi.[64] The Intercantonal Society of Jura Industries (SIIJ), a newly formed trade association for watchmakers that represented their collective interests, selected Jacques David. David and Gribi had specific instructions from the SIIJ: "make a serious and detailed study of the organization, tools, financial situation and in general any other aspect of American watch factories."[65]

The young Jacques David was an early advocate of using machines to produce watches and served as an engineer, making him a natural and convenient choice. After a ten-day voyage, David arrived in New York aboard the *Amerique* on August 23, 1876, and proceeded onto Philadelphia, almost exactly halfway through the Centennial Exhibition's run.[66]

Jacques David, shown later in life. He was 31 in 1876. From "La Patrie Suisse," No. 500, 1912 (Public Domain).

With his arrival, David and Gribi, embarked on their mission, one that would be essential to the future survival of their industry and the Swiss national economy. These two unsuspecting watchmakers were about to become industrial spies, playing a critical part in the transformation of Swiss watchmaking, one that would change the history of the global watch industry forever.[67]

Chapter 2:

A New Kind of Company

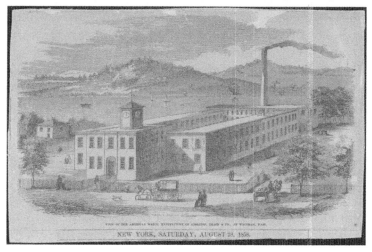

NEW YORK, SATURDAY, AUGUST 28, 1858.

Early Waltham factory shown in 1858 (Digital Commonwealth, Public Domain)

"[The watch industry] which stagnated for three centuries in an undeveloped condition, and which had been disintegrated for the last hundred years, was now for the first time brought into an all connected and perfectly-organized system."[68]

-Appleton's Journal, in an article about Waltham, 1870

Boston – 1850

Waltham's founding and early failure

Waltham was founded by Aaron L. Dennison in 1850 when he decided to pursue a vision for making watches by machine. The idea was so novel at the time that his co-owners tried to disguise the real intent to avoid being mocked.[69] Dennison was a skilled traditional watchmaker but was also inspired by machines becoming prevalent in many American industries, especially in firearms production.[70] Making watches by machine would require precision parts that were tens or hundreds of times smaller than those in a firearm. The idea was truly novel and unsurprising that it provoked public ridicule. It seemed to be general knowledge that the intricacies of watchmaking required the skilled artisans of Switzerland.

Dennison benefitted from the clock industry in New England, which had developed substantially under Eli Terry. In 1807, Terry began a quest to make 4,000 clocks. He developed a method and machinery to mass-produce clocks, allowing them to become ubiquitous in America. As noted by Landes, "It was this factory that showed for the first time that mass production of timepieces was feasible and profitable."[71]

One of Terry's proteges was Chauncey Jerome, who in 1837 sought to mass produce a brass clock instead of the earlier wooden models. Applying the same principles of mass production, Jerome made 40,000 brass clock movements at $1.40 each.[72] Dennison's American predecessors tried to carry the concept to watchmaking in the 1830s and 1840s, but none succeeded.[73]

Dennison found the gap between making watches by hand and mass production methods using machines was immense. Even moving from hand tools to human assistive devices that provided consistent precision would have vastly improved capability. Dennison's original idea was to manufacture parts using assistive tools or small machines using skilled watchmakers to operate them and assemble the final product. The idea was considered novel since many watchmakers worked alone and produced every part themselves. However, the system was too expensive to be practical.[74] His machines were neither automatic nor was the company able to make watches in the quantity required to create financially suitable economies of scale.[75] Dennison's machines were nowhere near the later ingenuity of the automatic screw machine shown at the Centennial Exhibition.

Under Dennison, the early company produced watches that required about eighteen person-days of labor to construct, or twice as long as it took the Swiss.[76] Labor in America was also more expensive than in Switzerland, meaning each Dennison watch required more labor at a higher wage. Therefore, Dennison's factory produced less efficiently and more expensively and generally provided the same product as the Swiss.

Dennison's watches were no more affordable than the era's luxury Swiss and English timepieces, and willing vendors were in short supply.[77] One of Dennison's former partners surmised that Dennison made no noticeable contribution to the design of watches, taunting, "now tell us watchmakers wherein can you discover any improvement in the construction…made or introduced by [Dennison]?"[78]

Then in 1856, an economic panic quickly dampened any headway the company made. As customers disappeared, Dennison could not sell his inventory.[79] Dennison's Waltham was broke, entering bankruptcy liquidation in 1857.[80] In the later words of Royal Robbins, Dennison demonstrated the "practicability of making watches by machinery but not enough to show the [profit] advantage of that method."[81]

Royal Robbins purchases Waltham

It was in 1857 that Robbins entered the annals of Waltham's history. Contrary to Dennison, Robbins was a professional businessman with the tact and shrewdness to build a failed company into an integrated manufacturing, sales, and marketing empire that would transform the vast international watch industry within fifteen years. In 1857, Robbins was a single bachelor, thirty-three years old, and had amassed a fortune worth $140,000.[82] He began working for his uncle at seventeen, learning the watch export business at *Robbins & Martin* in Birmingham, England. When the company dissolved, Robbins started his own watch import business in New York in 1846.[83]

When Robbins heard about Waltham's pending bankruptcy auction, he formed a new business partnership that would bid on Dennison's insolvent watch company. While Robbins understood the jewelry sales and distribution business, he knew nothing about watch production.[84] He joined two other investors: Eliashab Tracy and Theodore Baker, both watchcase makers, who at least knew something about manufacturing.[85] It gave Robbins the chance to invest in a novel concept: watchmaking by machinery, with the opportunity to gain immense wealth should the venture succeed. Robbins intended to provide two-thirds of the financial capital; Baker would run the factory.[86]

According to Dennison's brother, "Mr. Robbins being a shrewd businessman saw the [seeds] of a great business in the affair and instead of stopping at the [agreed upon bidding limit] bid on to more than double the [agreed upon amount]."[87] Robbins committed the trio to a $56,000 investment for the bankrupt folly, which Robbins claimed was "much to [his partners'] alarm and disgust."[88]

The trouble began the day of the purchase. The night before the auction and the night after, a supposed company creditor removed most of the machinery. With Robbins unaware of the loss, Waltham was stripped of most of the assets, causing the trio to unknowingly purchase an almost-machineless factory.[89] Robbins would later recall: "We found we had got the wooden buildings, but not much besides"[90] and later continuing, "most of what little machinery there was and most of the [watches] in process which we thought we had bought, had been carried off the night before the sale, and the balance the night after."[91]

The troubles did not stop there. Within a few short months, Baker and Tracy abandoned Robbins, leaving him to run the company in a manufacturing industry he knew nothing about.[92] Robbins later recalled Tracy and Baker's abandonment during a speech: "Tracy & Baker, perhaps sniffing the financial storm just ahead [of the Panic of 1857], abandoned all the capital, some $15,000 they had put into the venture, and in fact abandoned, by agreement, the whole enterprise to me."[93]

With Baker and Tracy gone and the purchase stripped of most of its assets, Robbins had no choice but to move to Boston and personally oversee his investment. Robbins stated: "[I] found myself, much against my will, obliged not only to take an active part in the management but [also] to put more money in."[94]

Robbins never forgot Tracy and Baker and bitterly recounted their abandonment. Thirteen years later, in a letter to shareholders, he crossed out the original text of "Baker & Tracy successfully retired in the autumn of that year" and made it spitefully read "Baker & Tracy success~~fully~~*ively* retired *disappointed losers* in the autumn of [1857] and [I] as the only remaining partner continued the business..."[95]

Robbins had little to show until the arrival of Ambrose Webster in the spring of 1857. As horology historian Richard Watkins noted, Robbins "knew even less about machinery than watchmaking and, either by sheer luck or a stroke of genius, he employed Ambrose Webster as his head mechanic; he was the first machinist hired."[96] Webster understood the value of interchangeability, having worked at the Springfield Armory where interchangeable parts for firearms were developed and improved.

Webster would become one of Waltham's most storied employees. He was the mastermind of the semi-automated processes and interchangeability that Waltham would eventually achieve, including the initiation of standard measurement sizes for tooling.[97] Before Webster, automation at Waltham's factory was nonexistent and discouraged.[98] With Webster's arrival, Waltham began inventing the production machines it needed that would soon lead to unimagined production efficiency and profitability.

Waltham's march to profitability

One of Robbins' first business decisions was to sell what he could to generate cash. He had inherited some work-in-progress and watch parts, which the company quickly assembled and began to sell about 900 watches under the name *Appleton, Tracy, & Co (AT&C)*, which was both the name of the company at the time, and the watch. The watches were of high to moderate quality, but Robbins used his pricing knowledge to set both a fair and firm price. He used his experience from his distribution company, *Robbins & Appleton* to get the watches into circulation, immediately overcoming one of Dennison's obstacles. By September 1857, his retail network was distributing 150 watches per month, a 50% increase over Dennison. The network extended from Boston to New York to Philadelphia and expanded west via St. Louis.[99]

That September, just as Robbins began to develop his distribution network, economic panic returned to the United States. The Panic caused the fledgling enterprise to incur four straight months of losses as sales diminished to twenty watches per month.[100] In Robbins' words, the "general panic, never equaled before or since" dried up demand as merchants "were falling in every direction."[101]

Faced with a growing financial crisis and having assumed ownership of Waltham at potentially one of the worst times of the era, Robbins later admitted that the first few months of ownership consumed his money and he was in debt.[102] Realizing he was on the verge of financial failure less than six months after purchasing the factory, Robbins called an all-hands meeting of employees, offering an option – they could sacrifice together, or the factory would shut down. He told them: "rather than shut down I would make an effort to run through the Spring [of 1858] if they would accept half pay." Every employee accepted the offer.[103]

As the Panic progressed, Robbins knew he needed to sell a product that a depressed economy would buy, which meant he needed to reduce the cost of the watch to make it attractively affordable. He began using inventory as collateral for loans and traveling to auctions to sell any watches he could to generate badly needed cash. In the middle of the recession, he counter-cyclically invested heavily in the development of machinery to bring down the average costs of production, a move that would have seemed unwise given the circumstances and track record of the company.[104]

During this time, the young maverick Ambrose Webster started to reorient the whole company to value the machine shop, which produced the company's novel machinery, making it the competitive advantage of the firm rather than a supporting agency.[105] Robbins also incentivized employees to improve their processes, paying them for what they produced rather than by the day. This encouraged and rewarded employees for developing new machines and methods that ultimately enhanced efficiency. By 1858, Waltham could produce a watch in 3.4 person-days, making the company now twice as efficient as the Swiss.[106] Waltham quickly cut the variable cost of production of a watch by 50%.[107]

Stumbling onto a new market segment

Robbins needed a watch cheaper than the *AT&C* that would sell in a recession. In the winter of 1858, the company was almost $10,000 in debt and desperately needed a product to generate quick sales.[108] The company developed the *P.S. Bartlett (PSB)*, which looked very similar to the previous model,[109] but had fewer parts and cost 25% less. The *PSB* proved an immediate success. Robbins had inadvertently discovered immense demand for cheap but reliable watches among American consumers; the cheaper *PSB* was now the consumer's model of choice.[110]

Robbins' experience in the distribution business solved the most pressing point of Waltham's early failure: distribution, sales, and marketing. Robbins had the channels to distribute his reliable but inexpensive watches, aided by a growing railroad network in a recovering economy. In mid-1858, Waltham had approximately 100 retail outlets through its network of jewelers. Six months later, that doubled to over 200 jewelers. The company obtained its first positive net cash position in August, 1858.[111]

The near-financial ruin that Robbins suffered led him to diversify some of his financial risk. In September 1858, Robbins conducted a company restructuring to bring in investors, which showed how far he had come in a short year and a half in demonstrating the potential of mass-produced watches. Robbins had turned his purchase of Waltham into a return of $175,000 in just over a year while personally knowing almost nothing about the mechanized production of watches.[112] He increased the number of employees from 110 in September to 180 by the end of 1858.[113]

At the close of the year, Robbins wrote his first report to investors, noting: "the sales of our [watches] exceed each month our production & at the rate they are progressing will soon exhaust our stock. The last two or three months my attention has been constantly taken up with the enlargement of our works & the increasing of our machinery tools & hands to meet the demands upon us."[114] He increased the factory, tools, and employees by

70% and changed the company's name to the American Watch Company, the legal name it would hold going forward. However, the company would colloquially become known for its physical location in the town of Waltham.

The soldier's watch

After the early success of the relatively cheap *PSB* watch, Robbins chose to maintain the company's focus on the most demanded segment of the market: low-priced goods. He wrote to his investors in 1862: "The demand as [of] yet is for low priced goods...consequently we are paying special attention to the manufacture of such, on which the profit will be small."[115] Waltham had a virtual monopoly on the lower-priced segment as the only maker of affordable, reliable machine-made watches, producing around 15,000 watches per year.[116] There was no competition, and demand was high.

While the *PSB* was cheaper than traditional luxury watches, it was affordable to very few customers of the era. In 1861, Waltham introduced an even cheaper watch: the *Ellery*. While it still commanded about two months' pay for a private in the Union Army, it was steadfast and unique when compared to the cheap Swiss watches selling within the same price category. During a time of war when over one million soldiers were in military service, this affordable watch quickly became known as the "Soldier's Watch." It was in a class of its own compared to other options available to consumers at the time. At wholesale, it only cost $13, or about $25 at retail, a significant amount of money, but it was the only watch near that price point that was considered reliable. [117] By comparison, other dependable watches of the era could cost more than twice as much.

The *Ellery* offered reliable timekeeping to an entirely new segment of consumers even though knowing the exactness of the hour was yet of little consequence to most people in the early 1860s. In prior decades, it would not have been unusual for officers from the wealthy class to own an expensive watch and track the time. There were numerous examples of Civil War soldiers of all ranks and grades buying watches and genuinely caring about them.[118] Two months' pay might seem unaffordable to a soldier, but evidence from the era strongly suggests that soldiers bought the *Ellery* anyway.

Author of the book *The Appreciation and Authentication of Civil War Timepieces*, Clint Geller found that most of the *Ellery* and *PSB* watches he examined (and could be traced to specific Civil War soldiers via their inscriptions), were purchased by or presented to enlisted soldiers. Conversely, he found that Waltham watches presented to commissioned officers were of the company's two highest grades: the *AT&C* and the *American Watch Co (AWC)*, Waltham's best watch. The *Ellery* was by no means the least expensive of all watches on the market, but it was nevertheless priced within the means of enlisted soldiers. Thus, in Geller's research, he found "copious evidence that large numbers of soldiers were willing to pay far more than the cost of the cheapest available watch to be able to take what they regarded as a reliable watch into harm's way."[119]

Waltham's focus on the affordable market could be seen in the Civil War-era advertisements. The advertisements sent two consistent messages: 1)

Waltham made a *reliable* watch that 2) was much *cheaper* than other available Swiss watches:

"Beware of Counterfeits... A genuine Waltham Watch costs less to buy and will last much longer than foreign made watches of the same quality" (1862).[120]

"Buy a genuine Waltham Watch if you want a durable and a reliable time-keeper...it costs less and is worth double the price of these worthless English and Swiss watches" (1863).[121]

The *Ellery* became the embodiment of 'cheap' and 'reliable.' It far exceeded the expectation of customers who previously had few, if any, options for a personal watch. Robbins concluded his remarks to investors in 1862 by writing that "trade will *not soon demand* the better and even the best goods we produce" (author's emphasis).[122]

The *Ellery* and *PSB* soon accounted for almost 80% of Waltham's revenue. Meanwhile, Waltham's luxury watches contributed less than 1% of revenue.[123] The success of the company was driven by the affordable segment. In 1864, Robbins reported that his biggest problem was that "demand for our productions continues not only without abatement but in quantities we find ourselves wholly unable to supply."[124]

Robbins boasted that Waltham had "made more money than I had reason to expect we should."[125] This resulted in significant profits, with margins reaching an average of 38% for the five years that encompassed the Civil War.[126] Even when adjusted for wartime inflation, Waltham's profits grew from $21,000 in 1860 to $251,000 in 1865 (adjusted to 1860 dollars).[127] That year, Robbins took home $172,000 (adjusted to 1860 dollars), making him the highest taxpayer in Boston.[128]

Robbins had positioned Waltham with technological innovation and by accurately identifying what the market demanded. As the Civil War was ending, he wrote to investors:

> *I may safely congratulate you not only on the past but on the prospects of the future for our works. We have now so much capital, so much reputation and popularity in fact so solid and broad a basis that I dismiss for my part all apprehension for the future come what will financially and politically to the general public.*[129]

Seeds of competition

Waltham's immense profits were bound to invite American competitors, and the battle lines of industrial combat were drawn. The most detracting seeds of competition were sown in 1864 with the establishment of the Elgin National Watch Company, whose investors were drawn into the market by the outsized growth of Waltham's profits. Elgin's founders raised $100,000 in capital in just a few months.

Once established, Elgin set about an aggressive recruitment campaign to entice Waltham's employees to leave Robbins and join the new entrepreneurial venture, including P.S. Bartlett himself. In total, Elgin secured seven key recruits that brought with them enough institutional knowledge to establish a competitor factory by 1865.[130] This also catalyzed a trend in which imitators began producing and using machines like Waltham's. Even Jacques David later reported: "The American machines are very similar from one factory to another, because they all are more or less copied from those at Waltham, which carried out most of the tests and paid for most of the experiments."[131]

Competition in the market necessitated burgeoning trade secrecy practices. In the 1860s and 1870s, the easy transfer of trade secrets was possible because Waltham relied upon trade secrecy for its machinery innovation, almost exclusively, for the first twenty-five years of its operation. It was not until after the Centennial Exhibition that Waltham patented some of its machines, with the first patent probably being filed in 1882.[132] Even the impressive automatic screw machine was not patented. This might seem odd, but there were a few practical reasons for this.

First, many machine improvements were happening so fast that a patent could quickly become obsolete. Professor Dan Clawson found in his research that most improvements in industrial-era companies like Waltham "were a kind of 'minor' tinkering that never [got] patented, and yet [they were] a crucial part of continuing improvements in productivity."[133]

Second, patents incurred an administrative and financial burden to file, yet a patent on a watchmaking machine provided no corresponding marketing advantage. Waltham never advertised *how* its watches were made except that they were made by machine, so there was no advantage to patenting a machine for this purpose. On the other hand, a watch with a patented design was something the customer could buy. By the time of the Centennial, Waltham would hold fifteen patents, all in watches, nine of which were invented by Charles Vander Woerd, the inventor of the automatic screw machine.[134] David noted watch patents as a significant advantage for Waltham's advertising.[135]

Finally, filing a patent required disclosing one's design, which could then be legally altered and produced by competitors. The machine designs would eventually leak out by relying on trade secrecy, but would take longer than public disclosure through a patent.[136] Business historian Alfred Chandler, writing about the era observed: "Unpatented proprietary knowledge, 'trade secrets,' and broad product-specific knowledge and experience created far more powerful barriers to entry than did patents."[137] Even in the modern era, research has shown that trade secrecy is preferred to patents in a majority of industries.[a] [138]

Even without patenting its machines, Waltham's productivity increased significantly relative to its competitors as employees were motivated to find efficiencies to improve production processes. Inventions of machines and processes at Waltham allowed the company to continuously improve its rate of production, thus reducing the cost per watch. This resulted in *exponential* improvement in production efficiency from 1857 to 1865.

Despite Waltham having a legitimate potential competitor in Elgin, Robbins viewed Waltham as having a monopoly, something he confidently flouted even after Elgin's founding. In 1865, the competition was not concerning; there was no reason to assume profit margins would become cutthroat or that a zero-sum game would emerge.

Robbins' confidence was bolstered by the increasing success of Waltham's watches in the market.

---

[a] A 1994 survey of thirty-three industries found that trade secrecy was the most preferred method for protecting inventions. The same research report found that patents were preferred by less than one quarter of industries.

He told investors that the company had "vastly increased [its] hold on the public preference during the last few years." Robbins signaled that he had no intent to throttle Waltham's growing production, as he was in pursuit of being the market's top producer of cheap, reliable watches.[139]

Fending off competition

By the close of 1870, at least ten other companies had joined the market at some point throughout the previous decade.[140] The smooth flow of American capital to industrial competitors began to take a toll on Waltham, who started to maintain a vigilant observance of competitive threats. Robbins informed shareholders that "The Competition from other factories [has] of course somewhat lessened our profits as they have interfered with our substantial monopoly."[141]

Waltham's sensitivity to the competition was evident in its advertising expenditures which were 1.4% of sales from 1865 to 1867 when the competition was minimal. Advertising tripled to 5.1% of sales from 1870 to 1872 when competition began to grow in earnest.[142] By 1874, the competition could not be ignored.[143] Waltham's accuracy, reliability, and warranty features, formerly found only in luxury watches, were now found in most American watches at most price points.

Since product differentiation became increasingly difficult among the plethora of competitors, Robbins regularly focused on remaining competitive by lowering unit production costs through improving economies of scale. This was a common strategy during the industrial revolution and could be found in almost every late nineteenth-century industry, from cigarettes to steel.[144]

As production quantities increased, Waltham needed to expand its market to absorb the increasing quantities of affordable watches. Robbins began to look internationally for new customers, precipitating the company's global focus. He reported that as early as 1867, Waltham's sales agents overlooked "nothing which may tend to enlarge the market for us. Earnest endeavours are [being made] in the western states, of which Chicago is the great center, on the Pacific Coast and in Canada to establish on a permanent foundation not only our trade but our reputation as the leading watchmakers." He added, "every day brings proof that we are adding very surely to our celebrity as well as to the popularity of our watches."[145]

In 1875, the company began making goods specifically for foreign markets. By the time of the Centennial Exhibition, Waltham would sell watches as far as Australia, New Zealand, India, Japan, and Russia, with international sales accounting for 25% of revenue.[146] Robbins informed shareholders: "We are very much encouraged by the favor with which our goods are being received outside of the United States. It now really appears as if we should at no distant time compete successfully for the watch trade in the markets of all nations."[147]

A company transformed

In every respect, Waltham was transformed under Robbins both as a manufacturing company and a business. Within twenty years of his purchase, Robbins and his company would garner the admiration of

American customers and dignitaries worldwide. Abraham Lincoln owned a Waltham watch and President Ulysses S. Grant would visit the Waltham factory in 1876; even the Chinese Ambassador paid respects during a visit to the novel company as early as 1864.[148]

Later in the nineteenth century, after Waltham presumably achieved a higher level of automation, the avid watch enthusiast Henry Ford would visit the factory and find inspiration from Waltham for his revolutionary automobile assembly line. Henry Ford II, Ford's grandson and the CEO of the Ford Motor Company, later recounted:

> *I think - I always understood...[Henry Ford] got the idea from the Waltham Watch Company originally by seeing watches going down on an assembly line and he felt that [technique] could be applied to the manufacture of automobiles. There are some other stories prevalent, but that is the one I always heard. So that is the one I believe to be the truth.[149]*

Despite Robbins' ability to quickly turn Waltham around out of Dennison's failure, it was Dennison who would gain much of the future credit for Waltham's success, including having a much higher profile than Robbins well into the modern era. While not a good businessman, Dennison understood the importance of personal image in the public eye, especially after leaving Waltham. Even during Robbins' own lifetime, Dennison would self-aggrandize the title 'Father of American Watchmaking,' a designation that has appeared in written accounts ever since. But some of his contemporaries would passionately dispute this aggrandizement, with one writing: "[Dennison's] claim to be the sole Father of American watch-making is a position, it is believed, that neither he nor his friends can establish."[150]

Chapter 3:

The Most Remarkable Factory Ever Built

Aaron Dennison (left) and Royal E. Robbins (Right), two very different men, both in appearance, management, and vision for watch production (Abbott, 1908, Public Domain)

Waltham Factory – May 1876

By 1876, Robbins' factory had grown to employ almost 1,000 workers and could produce 105,000 watches a year with an average wholesale price of just over $9. His factory was lauded by contemporaries for its environment and was known for its treatment of both men and women workers. While the factories of the era were often known for their mistreatment of workers, sources of the period and subsequent research indicate Waltham was a laudable employer whose workers led to its storied success (though a discussion on the reliability and consistency of sources will conclude this chapter).

It was within the factory walls that Waltham's culture encouraged innovative improvements to both machines and production processes, enabling people with little knowledge of watchmaking to produce the world's most reliable timekeepers. One noteworthy example was Eliza Jane Putnam, whose name hardly survives in any records. She was not remarkable; instead, she represented the ordinary Waltham employee, 40% of which were women. She worked at the factory and would one day represent Waltham as part of its exhibit at the Centennial.

She was a single 30-year-old woman. She lived at 63 Adams Street in the company's namesake town, which numbered around 10,000 people. She had worked at the watch factory since October of 1874. She had no formal experience and probably knew nothing about traditional watchmaking. The official report from the Centennial Exhibition, whose judges would have seen Putnam working at Waltham's exhibit, noted that the employees of Waltham were: "in total ignorance of the fundamental principles upon which the performance of a watch depends."[151]

With a tone of condescension and bewilderment, Jacques David observed: "The mechanical system of manufacture adopted in America enables the factories to employ many people who know nothing of the watch industry. They ask that their workmen and women be conscientious, intelligent enough to be interested in their work and to have the capacity to understand it. That is enough for the majority of men and women employed on the machines, but these qualities are absolutely essential."[152]

Early approaches to equality in the workplace

Putnam quickly proved herself as a strong operator deserving above-average pay.[153] She earned about $1.60 per day during most months in 1874 to 1875, giving her an annual compensation of $488. Using a simple inflation conversion, this equates to about $11,000 in 2017, but given the relative wages and associated *prestige value* or economic status, Putnam's wages were the modern equivalent of $150,000 annually.[154]

While this might seem inordinately high for such a simple task as operating a mostly automatic machine, Waltham's machines required familiarization, training, and learned efficiency. There was a value to maintaining an employee; the machines of the 1870s required much less skill than those of the 1860s, but still benefitted from a skilled operator that cost the company time to train. By 1890, the machines would be fully automatic with handling systems and required very little skill, but this stereotypical mindless, Gilded Age factory work was still a decade or more away from Putnam's present job. In 1876, most jobs in the factory were at least semi-skilled, except for some support positions.[155]

Robbins viewed Waltham's workers as an asset that led to profitability through investment in their work. He told the shareholders in 1871 that the key to profitable business was not cutting costs through low wages, but rather the "contentment and prosperity on the part of the workmen as the result in part of an individual interest ·in the business."[156] To ensure employees were invested in the company's success, Robbins allowed employees to buy shares in the company, of which 203 (40%) employees subscribed in 1870.[157]

Giving stock ownership to the employees was a generous inducement as the company paid dividends of around 20% annually.[158] David would observe: "Several employees and workmen from Waltham have truly made their fortune and have retired, encouraging others by their example."[159] In one research study conducted on Waltham's wages during the Civil War, labor economist Howard Gitelman noted: "We may tentatively conclude that Waltham Watch offered higher wages than most firms through the war period."[160]

By 1876, Waltham observed a policy of equal pay for equal work by men and women. The official report from the judges at the Centennial Exhibition noted: "the amount of wages paid by the company is determined by the skill and experience required, not by the sex of the operatives."[161] Labor reformer John Swinton, visiting in 1887, claimed this policy was "rigidly observed."[162] Even David noted that while women's wages were generally lower, women were paid the same as men for many jobs.

While this was the company's policy, it was not true in practice as the average pay for men still exceeded that of women as noted by both David in 1876 and later by Swinton in 1887.[163] Much of this had to do with how women were employed in the factory: "The work to which the softer sex are assigned is always of a lighter character and much of it is very dainty and delicate, requiring keen eyes and deft fingers, but neither trying to the mind nor injurious to the body."[164] Putnam earned a higher wage than most of her counterparts, but it was still below that of the average man, who made $2.43.[165]

The women of Waltham were described as professionals and a lynchpin of the factory's success. Their work environment was lauded by David, who described a setting that did not meet many later stereotypes of industrial-era factories, primarily the collegial working conditions and the inventive freedom of the employees. David described the women as: "always very neat and their clothing, although simple, is often elegant. Hairstyles are in fashion, and flowers, collars, brooches and rings are frequently worn."[166]

Factory life

After arriving at work, Putnam would have assumed her station at a long wooden table, sitting alongside ten to twenty of her co-workers with some benches overlooking the Charles River. The factory was not an insult to the dignity of the workers: "there is nothing that suggests the usual close and sunless dinginess of the manufactory…Windows, opening at all points of the compass, let in floods of light, [and] give access to the fresh breezes" wrote the widely read *Appleton's Journal* during an 1870 tour.[167]

As noted by David, the factory had gas lights, a ventilation system, bathrooms, cloakrooms, watering stations, well-lit offices, and workshops with attractive furniture. David remarked, "you could find none better and no expense has been spared;" the workshops were immaculately clean.[168] In some departments, such as the pinion department where Putnam worked, women made up the majority of the workers and it was not uncommon to find personal framed pictures of the employees' families adorning the walls amidst flowers creating an inviting ambiance.[169]

Inside the Waltham Factory in the late 19th Century (W.A. Webster, American Waltham Watch Factory, Public Domain)

A complex factory like Waltham presented numerous opportunities for accidents. Heavy metal machines could easily trap and crush a limb with little or no warning. In his reports to shareholders, Robbins demonstrated a concern for safe working conditions at the expense of the company. In 1874, during the most difficult years of the Panic of 1873, the company abandoned and rebuilt part of the factory because of its "dilapidation and insecurity." The rebuilding was "absolutely necessary" to ensure the factory could operate with "safety and convenience" and because some parts of the factory had become "unduly crowded."[170]

Output in each department was governed by a foreman, who supervised the twenty to forty workers in his shop, set and paid their wages, and was responsible for the quantity and quality of output. The foreman was a manager with wide latitude over the conditions and operations within the department.[171] They often hired and fired their employees. As historian Peter Stearns noted, during the industrial revolution: "[the foremen] were expected to represent management interests and to drive their workers hard...For the first time in Western history (aside from American slavery), a growing minority of people were working under the daily control of someone else, and not simply for a few years of youthful apprenticeship but for a lifetime."[172]

Life in the town of Waltham

Hard work in the factory resulted in well-earned leisure. The Swiss cobbler and Centennial delegation member Edward Bally noted: "The American works like a clock...Saturday afternoon, he is free; he puts his household in order, so as to be able to go on Sunday morning to church, and on Sunday afternoon, to take his family for a trip by railroad, or by steamboat. On this occasion, he indulges in a mug of beer, or a glass of wine."[173]

Waltham workers enjoyed community gatherings including bicycle, canoe, and literary clubs, with there being "no lack of social entertainments for the leisure hours of the people."[174] Many workers in the factory took active roles in promoting community events including picnics, baseball leagues, dances, festivals, ice-skating, sleigh rides, and musicals.[175] Gitelman observed: "The watch workers were, if anything, a singularly gregarious social group. Within the company, they organized leisure-time entertainments and a variety of self-help and self-improvement activities...They displayed an élan and an activism that made them attractive to one another and to outsiders as well."[176]

At Robbins' behest, Waltham provided the local area with recreational facilities, dining rooms, housing facilities, well-kept parks and avenues, pristine factory conditions, and public transportation to the surrounding areas. When confronted about the expenditures, Robbins replied that it was extremely profitable, not only because of "the delight an employer should feel in providing for his employes the best practical conditions of labor, [but] it is clearly [in] his best interest" to do so.[177] Swinton, visiting the factory in 1887, concluded: "In short, Mr. Robbins claims that he serves his Company best when he secures at any expense a willing and contented service from his employes."[178]

Robbins' view of work and workers

Robbins employed many people with physical disabilities, with one contemporary writing: "there are many individuals who are not in the enjoyment of vigorous health [who]...find work [at the factory] which is within their ability."[179] Robbins even pre-dated modern reserve military duty employment laws by a century. According to a company publication, at the outbreak of the Civil War, "men who were valuable to [Waltham] by reason of their skill and experience were not...dissuaded from offering their services to their country in its hour of peril and need, but were urged to enlist in the Army, with the promise of employment on their return."[180] There was a reputable claim that Robbins made good on his war-time service guarantee and employed a severely wounded veteran as a janitor because he could no longer operate the machinery, yet Robbins still paid him his former watchmaker's wages.[181]

More than twenty years after the war, Waltham employee E.A. Marsh wrote: "A stranger would be impressed in observing the employees as they leave the factory, by the number of persons walking with the aid of a cane, others needing crutches, and still others having but one arm...the unusual number of lame and halt who are here gathered is explained by the fact that many veterans of the war are still employed."[182]

This period of history was plagued by worker exploitation, poor working conditions, and mindless work with demanding requirements. Even Waltham had demanding expectations of workers. Waltham's system of rigid output was ruthless and unforgiving, with David noting: "Those who do not work with their head as well as with their fingers are outdone and discarded."[183] David also wrote: "The least voluntary negligence or defect in intelligence or activity causes immediate dismissal."[184] Despite this expectation of workers, David suggested that Waltham's environment favored the promotion of innovation and teamwork over rigidity.[185]

Waltham's working conditions and managerial practices naturally led to the innovation of process improvements. Waltham's workers were free to invent new methods and new technologies since they were not eliminating their artisanal job, but rather just redefining their manufacturing job more efficiently. In other words, the workers viewed innovation as a friend that could "halve the cost of the watch, but will not halve their wages, and will make their services still more valuable to the Company."[186] Thus the Swiss noted that

American workers toiled "unceasingly to simplify the manipulation, to invent and to apply every possible improvement."[187]

David observed that American factory workers constantly sought to advance their products and production methods. He wrote:

> ...the whole or part of the ownership of the idea, the patent or the benefit resulting from application to the factory or sale to other factories of the invention or patented improvement, returns to the workman and inventive employee...Their process of constant improvement led to efficiency and continuously reduced costs of production.[188]

Managerial innovation

The quickly growing workforce and scalable production required a different type of innovation: improving managerial practices to manage a factory with 1,000 employees that would quickly grow to 2,000 and beyond. It was only managerial innovation in watchmaking that made this growth of the workforce possible. Waltham's ability to implement systems of control for this large of an organization was not entirely novel but far from widespread in American business of the era. David observed the modular structure used in the watch factories:

> Work is carried out in a number of workshops which are under the direction and monitoring of heads of department or foremen. There are 15 to 20 of these departments in the large establishments...The foreman or workshop head is responsible to the two directors and

the board of directors for the observation of regulations by himself and all the people in his department.[189]

As the largest watchmaking factory, Waltham managed a quickly growing organization through modularization that promoted inventive exploration. David felt this system gave foremen latitude to be inventive and operate with decentralized control. But he also noted certain regulations that governed the broader organization to ensure efficiency: "While having, to a large degree, the right to take initiatives, each foreman must observe certain rules when he believes it is his duty to introduce any improvement, so that everyone is warned of this improvement and all departments can contribute to it."[190]

150 years of hindsight

Waltham's working conditions might seem surprising or even unbelievable given most of what modern historians know about the Gilded Age. While contrary to the prevailing conditions found in most factories, Waltham's conditions were verified by numerous respectable and independent sources.

First, the company's literature and accounts written by employees across decades show a progressive company for the era, though biased accounts would be expected. Supporting these claims came David's 1876 report, writing: "In Waltham especially, we were struck by the cleanliness of the city, the elegance of the majority of the houses, and the good appearance of everything."[191] By his own account, David did not rely on company literature but spoke with employees and saw the factory for himself.

Then there was Swinton's 1887 report, which further substantiated David's and other accounts. Swinton was a well-known labor and social reformer of his era and former editor of the New York Times. He was known for "openly indict[ing] the country's wealthy industrialists as the oppressors of laborers," as noted in the journal of Labor History.[192] Labor historian Frank Reuter observed that Swinton's regularly published paper always had "Colorful reports of the wretched living and factory conditions of workers…Wages, hours, factory and mine accidents, tenement conditions, child and women's labor, and unsanitary ventilation in mills were also discussed."[193] Swinton knew both Karl Marx and Samuel Gompers, and was a "staunch supporter" of Henry George.[194] He was known for having a skeptical eye towards factories and wealthy owners, making his account, perhaps, the most reliable of all.

During his visit to Waltham, Swinton both slept and ate in workers' housing. He found Waltham unique, noting there was a "presence here of a spirit wholly different from that crushed and cringing spirit which you often see in other factories." He continued: "There is here a measure of cooperation such as I have seen nowhere else between employes and employers. They strive to promote each other's interests and only those who are behind the scenes in a great manufacturing establishment can comprehend the extent to which the common prosperity may be thus promoted."[195]

Labor economist Howard Gitelman, writing for the Journal of Economic History with a century of hindsight, reported: "No information to the contrary – no complaints about supervisors or the pace of work –

has been found."[196] Gitelman spent a large portion of his career looking into the labor practices in the town of Waltham. He concluded that the labor experience in the town of Waltham was "untypical" because the locale was "shaped by so exemplary a firm as Waltham Watch."[197]

When considering other industrial-era factories, Waltham deserved the moniker espoused by Swinton as "one of the most remarkable industrial establishments ever built." This attracted a workforce who collaborated to develop the most novel system of watch manufacturing yet seen in the late nineteenth century.

Chapter 4:

Swiss Farmers and Watchmakers

Swiss factory town near the watchmaking regions circa 1890 (Library of Congress, Public Domain)

"On the lake's northern banks, are bright villages, handsome country seats, and scores of terraced vineyards. The Jura hills upon the north and the Savoy mountains on the south compose a panorama of picturesqueness seldom surpassed. Mount Blanc, though forty miles away, adds his majestic splendor to the scene."

-Samuel Byers, American Consul to Switzerland, 1875

Jura Region of Switzerland – May 1876

How the Swiss became watchmakers

The Swiss were not always known for watchmaking, nor were they always watchmakers. While they were the dominant producers of the global industry by 1840, they had oscillated through the preceding centuries producing both Genevan masterpieces and English counterfeits. For much of the eighteenth century, the Swiss watchmakers were the cheaper, outsourced labor for English and French watchmakers, serving a manufacturing role much like that of emerging economies in the late twentieth century.

Genevan masters produced objects of fine art while the much poorer cottage watchmakers of the countryside produced parts for the Genevans in addition to making, selling, and smuggling watches to France, England, and beyond. Yet by 1840, some of the Swiss watchmakers were producing the best watches in the world and had effectively silenced the previously-dominant industries of Germany, France, and England.[198] Historian David Landes noted: "By the second quarter of the nineteenth century, the Swiss mountain watch industry had swept all before it."[199]

The watch-producing regions were located in the French-speaking, mountainous areas of central and western Switzerland. In 1875, Samuel Byers, the United States' Consul and an accomplished author described the Swiss alpine villages as: "wooden towns, centuries of age, standing on the green, grassy slopes of mountain sides, or nestling close up in little vales and glens."[200] An 1842 English article described the region by noting the simple beauty of the watchmaking regions, as well as the poverty: "Notwithstanding the natural barrenness of the soil, and the bleakness of the climate, the country is now studded with beautiful and well-built villages, connected by easy communications; while the population are in the enjoyment, if not of great fortunes, at least of a happy and easy independence."[201]

The American government's representative wrote: "It is to be regretted that the labor of so worthy and industrious a people should have received so inadequate a reward, for in few parts of Europe have the earnings of the working-people been so poorly paid."[202] Consul Byers characterized the people and their year by writing that, "the summer, always short, is spent in cultivating a few potatoes, herding the goats, pressing the cheese, and cutting and carrying in the grass. The winter, always long, is spent in eating up the little that the summer gave, and in a struggle to keep from freezing. Here, as elsewhere in the country…[the people], notwithstanding their scanty rations and the sour wine, live long and heartily."[203]

While probably more apocryphal than reality, legend holds that a resident of one of these picturesque Alpine villages brought watchmaking to the region by accident in the late seventeenth century. Daniel JeanRichard was a young 14-years-old apprentice who was fascinated by the broken watch of a horse trader passing through the treacherous mountain region. He set out to fix the timekeeper and soon figured out how to craft an entire watch.[204]

He continued his work and found success making simple timepieces and his group of eager apprentices spread the trade to nearby towns, planting seeds of fine craftsmanship in an otherwise impoverished mountain region.[205] As the demand for watches spread, poor farmers and their families began to learn the trade, or at least how to make a few specific parts for a watch, which were then conglomerated by the watchmaker. Professor of economic geography Amy Glasmeier attributed "the long winters and poor quality of soils [that] restricted agriculture" to the growth of watchmaking in the region. These conditions created "the need for supplementary income...[which] upon receiving payment for [watch] parts, a farmer could reinvest the money he was paid in agricultural land or livestock."[206]

Farmers soon discovered that watchmaking paid better than farming; some became full-time watchmakers, while others farmed in the summer and made watch parts during the harsh winters.[207] By the late eighteenth century, many watch and parts makers had specialized into full-time producers, though the practice of part-time, supplemental work was still documented by 1875.[208]

A U.S. Government report from that year noted: "the peasant, when not actively engaged in agricultural pursuits, finds useful and profitable occupation in a hundred different ways, from felling timber on the mountains to making portions of the complicated and delicate works of watches."[209] Whether the story of young Daniel JeanRichard serving as the origin of watchmaking in the Jura is apocryphal or exact, the Jura mountains of Switzerland undoubtedly served as a cradle for the cottage industry of watchmaking by 1876.[210]

Another production center of even greater international fame was Geneva, which was known for producing the best watches. Since the sixteenth century, luxury watches had been produced in the city. To magnify their output and skirt guild regulations on labor, watchmakers began to contract out elements of production to farmers in the mountainous regions outside Geneva.[211] Historian Pierre-Yves Donzé suggested that this slow spread of watchmaking, driven by the 'invisible hand' of capitalism, was the more likely reason the cottage industry spread as far west as the mountain regions of the Jura.[212]

Regardless of origin, the vast majority of watchmaking in Switzerland was conducted by loosely organized, networks of peasant families who made individual pieces and parts for watches.[213] Orders for parts could not possibly be placed on demand as in a factory, rather, they were ordered seasonally in batches.

Marti described the process: starting with "one person, the establisseur, distributed the different tasks between a certain number of craftsmen who worked at home…He supplied the raw materials and saw (himself or through third parties) to the assembly of components that were made separately."[214] A family would make a part (somewhat in mass quantity) by hand, using various hand or bench tools. It took as many as 130 individual contributors of components to produce a Swiss watch. It required about one week of person-labor for the average watch and up to two years or more for the finest masterpiece.[215]

U.S. Consul Byers observed:

The work is performed in the people's homes and the workman is aided by his wife and children. Women, too, often learn the art… [the people of the Jura's] hands are the delicate machines and their own minds must be continually awake, to direct the hands aright. A Geneva watch-exporter may gather up the different parts of his watches from all

71

the different valleys [sic] of the Jura, and yet each part will be found to fit its special place with mathematical niceness, so careful and competent are the hands that have prepared the varied works.[216]

Swiss production innovation

Despite the Swiss reputation for making watches by hand, they had been leading innovators of production techniques for the last half-century, including the introduction of small assistive, human-driven apparatuses, typically called 'machines,' but distinctly different than what Waltham used. The major difference between the Swiss machines and Waltham's was that the Swiss tools assisted in production, while Waltham's machines took over most of the tasks entirely. Even though the Swiss' tools were not as advanced as Waltham's automated machines, they made production much more efficient than the century-old ways.

In 1839, the famed watchmaker Vacheron & Constantin began using tools that allowed it to roughly duplicate parts, but not with the precision found using Waltham machinery.[217] By 1840, the French manufacturers Japy & Fountainemellon were supposedly supplying the Swiss watch industry with an estimated 500,000 watch movements per year. Though the production numbers were probably a gross exaggeration,[b] this factory undoubtedly required the

---

[b] The factory would have required ~16,000 workers to produce watches at anywhere near the known efficiency capabilities of the era. This would make it over half the size of the entire watch industry and also the largest,

use of some type of mass production techniques to earn such a reputation.[218]

Contrary to the traditional way of watchmaking in Switzerland, David and Ernst Francillon of the Longines Watch Company were trying to do something revolutionary in Swiss watchmaking. Their goal was to create the first Swiss watchmaking factory. This would allow them to capitalize on the increased demand for timekeeping in developing markets. It was a concept that was iconoclastic to many who grew up making watches in their home. Most of the parts produced in a person's home lacked any sort of quality control and the absence of standard units of measure and communication between different producers of parts meant each piece required varying amounts of finishing and adjustment before the 130 or more pieces of a watch could fit together and tick properly. Francillon's idea was to bring watchmakers to the same building where they could better coordinate their products using small machines to aid the process.[219]

An American observer pointed out the obvious problem with the legacy Swiss system that led to poor quality and an infamous reputation: "one-third of all [handmade watch parts] are rejected as imperfect,

---

most organized factory of the era for almost a century to come. Managerial control of an enterprise this size was not seen until the railroad era in the United States. A factory even one-tenth this size ran completely counter to the culture as factories even greater than 500 workers were a rarity before 1900. If Japy used a disparate cottage network of producers, this would make it even more implausible. In the absence of a literal army of workers, Japy would have required technology that has not been found to have existed until around 1890. It would have also absorbed significant amounts of financial capital that the region consistently struggled to find. Japy would have also had to develop the machinery while also having none of the required technology bleed into the porous watchmaking regions and been put to use by others. Therefore, this nineteenth century claim is almost certainly apocryphal.

though they are still thrown together, covered with showy cases, and sent to distant markets." This resulted in a key flaw in such a precise and complex mechanical work: "the strength of a chain is determined by that of its weakest link, so the quality of a watch is determined by the accuracy of its least perfect part, one flaw vitiating the whole result."[220] Longines hoped that by bringing people together in a factory, it could eliminate some of the trial-and-error inherent in non-precision manufacturing.

The Longines approach was much different than Waltham's semi-automated factory. Longines simply gathered watchmakers together to simplify the artisanal process while investing in some early machines that made the work more efficient. The Centennial Awards Committee explained in its final report that, "while it is true that the application of labor-saving machines has been extensively introduced into watch manufacturing in Switzerland, yet it must be understood that these are of a very different character from those already mentioned in connection with the American system of manufacture."[221]

This was virtually the same conclusion reached by a group of Swiss watchmakers who had toured the Longines factory in 1875 when they concluded: "At Longines there are none of the complicated machines that are used in American factories; their real purpose is rather doubtful, especially [in Switzerland], where it is easy enough to find plenty of intelligent workers."[222]

Francillon and David experienced many significant challenges in setting up a factory in a culture dominated by independent craftsmen. Raising capital to support a factory proved difficult when most workers believed the work could and should be accomplished from home. Nor did Longines have the financial resources of American companies. Waltham raised equity (stock) over $2,000,000 due to the large availability of speculative American investors. On the other hand, Longines was forced to take a variety of bank loans and equity offerings, only raising the equivalent of $50,000 over ten years. It was hardly the capital necessary to establish a factory, invent machines, and experiment as Waltham was doing.[223]

Longines thought its system was novel compared to the traditional ways of watchmaking. However, once having seen Waltham's capability at the Centennial, David and Gribi were alarmed. The Centennial turned into a frightening embarrassment for Longines. All the sacrifice and capital spent to make its factory and machines a success was proving to be a decade too late; meanwhile, the company was almost bankrupt.

The evidence appeared clear to most: America had stolen the watch industry from the Swiss; their renowned artisanal trade was on the cusp of extinction.

Chapter 5:

Competing on the World's Stage

The Main Building of the Centennial Exhibition (Centennial Photographic Company, Public Domain)

Centennial Exhibition – July 1876

Once Robbins realized the initial success of his products, he did not view the Swiss as a real competitor. In the eyes of the consumer, they were selling completely different products. The affordable Swiss watch was considered little more than a cheap trinket that would assuredly break whereas closely priced

Waltham watches, such as the *Ellery*, were on par with the reliability and quality of a luxury Swiss watch. It was not just a perception, instead an inherent result of precision-machined parts which ensured "the accuracy and uniformity that machinery alone can confer."[224]

Nowhere in Waltham's annual reports from 1859 to 1876 did Robbins mention any concern about Swiss competition, instead only an unwavering confidence in Waltham's ability to surpass the Swiss. An 1871 Waltham advertisement claimed: "The finer qualities are as good as the best imported [Swiss watches] and the price on average is 20% less. The ordinary qualities so much surpass all ordinary imported watches as to render comparison of price impossible...Estimating price according to value – the Waltham watch has no competitor."[225] Waltham knew, and the customer perceived, that Waltham's watches were both cheaper and better.

Making the best watches in the world

Waltham's precision manufacturing of watch parts with nearly identical measurements provided a distinct advantage for the accuracy of construction. This also created the ability to use stronger and better materials than the Swiss in all grades of watches. Waltham's two huge steam engines drove the miles of shafts and belts which ran throughout the factory "and the result is the production of watches at the rate of one every three minutes, and with a uniformity and perfection which have at once and forever antiquated all previous methods of the production," wrote the Centennial judges.[226]

Waltham was aided by its location in New England with easy and cheap access to purified metals being processed in large quantities at regional foundries. Waltham invested in material science to exploit the advantages offered by using stronger metals. An 1884 English observation of the factory found a "systematic experimenting in tempering steel, in testing metals for their physical properties," which allowed the company to use science to select the best metals and processes.[227] Once the optimal materials were identified, high-quality metals could be used in even the cheapest Waltham watch.

Waltham's material selection and production capabilities standardized and simplified the long and arduous metal finishing process that precision performance parts such as balance springs required and traditionally had distinguished the good watches from the bad. For example, all of Waltham's watches, at all price points, used the same balance springs. The balance spring of the watch, which serves as a pacemaker, allows the balance wheel to rhythmically oscillate, which ultimately ensures the watch accurately tracks the time. Balance springs were made of tempered steel and often could make a watch extremely accurate and durable, or conversely, unreliable and prone to breakage. It was such a critical part that a reliable watch required a balance spring made with "the very best material," which had to be "evenly coiled, and must be so tempered as to secure a maximum degree of elasticity, and a continuance of this quality undiminished."[228]

Waltham's use of the same balance spring in all grades resulted in "movements which are of low price, and...perform often equal to the most carefully adjusted [watches]."[229] The official report from the Centennial's judges noted that Waltham's most common and ordinary watches performed with such accuracy that they exhibited characteristics of watches whose "cost would have necessarily increased tenfold."[230]

The Swiss handmade system brought a sharp contrast in the use of strong metals and durability. Better metals made the watch more durable against shocks and long-term usage. However, as the metals' quality, purity, and hardness increased, the more time and labor it took the watchmaker to form the parts and make them fit precisely. As the quality of a Swiss watch increased, so did the quality of the metals, the labor required, and the price.

The challenges of mass production

Stirring enough consumer demand to keep pace with Waltham's mass production presented a new challenge for the emerging mass-production industry. Society increasingly demanded watches, but not yet to the level that Waltham could produce. In the mid-1870s, the company faced the same problem that plagued the founder, Aaron Dennison: being able to sell what it could manufacture but on a much larger scale.

While Waltham could produce up to 105,000 watches a year, in 1876 it only sold 77,600 watches.[231] Sales of Waltham watches could not keep pace with the rate of the company's production improvements and efficiencies. To reach sustainable profitability, Robbins had to increase sales. Growing the factory and buying more machines did nothing without the ability to sell what the company could make.[232]

Waltham usually over-produced, leading to growing inventories. Thus, the factory shut down for weeks, sometimes more than a month at a time, including during the Centennial Exhibition, where the factory largely ceased operations in July and August of 1876. These shutdowns were typically pitched as vacation periods but were used to adjust production as well. A few years later, Robbins would call the vacations what they really were: "suspension of work in the summer (called vacation by courtesy)."[233] Thus, the factory frequently operated at about 80% of its annual capacity.

The marketing opportunity of a lifetime

As 1876 approached, the Centennial Exhibition provided a prescient opportunity to address the problems of insufficient demand and growing competition. At the Centennial, Robbins planned to do more than display watches in the typical showcase manner. Instead, he envisioned using the Centennial to capture the imagination of global markets and solidify Waltham's standing as an icon of quality and affordability, able to compete against even the most excellent Swiss producers. Robbins knew that many consumers doubted that a delicate watch could be manufactured by machine. The Centennial Exhibition would offer a brief six-month window to convey the validity of the Waltham system and its reputation to the world.

Robbins admitted to investors that he "hope[d] to make a show" at Philadelphia.[234] His letter to Waltham's shareholders in February 1876 gave an aura of a calculated strategy directed towards the Swiss watchmakers. His attention was not on the Swiss themselves nor challenging them head-on, rather he had a global focus – he wanted the customers of the world to realize Waltham's dominance of the Swiss *already*. Just as the broader Centennial Exhibition was focused on solidifying America's stature among the world powers, so did Waltham seek to demonstrate its rite of passage into dominance of the watch industry.[235]

Similar to leading modern companies that value opportunities to advance their product and reputation, usually through attention-earning creative methods, so too did Waltham. It spent over $15,000 on the Centennial Exhibition in addition to $30,000 expended on marketing in 1876. This combined $45,000, 6% of the company's total yearly budget, was massive and equaled Waltham's entire material expense to produce 84,000 watches that year.[236]

Waltham's calculated preparations began early and in earnest. Three months before the opening of the exhibition, the local newspaper wrote that Waltham's "skilled workmen have been engaged for some time in constructing a bench some thirty feet long and four wide, at each end of which will be a small Gothic building five by six feet with a studding of nine feet, finished in fancy wood veneers, making the whole a very ornamental and attractive sight."[237] This carpentry project was to become the base of the assembly line exhibit marveled by Gribi.

As for the machines, Robbins put calculated thought into the extent the exhibit would show long before the construction began in 1876. His letter of February 1st showed a well-planned display: "sixteen machines will be shown out of some thousands we make use of…we shall show only the process of making wheels and pinions."[238] This roster of machines would grow to twenty by May, including the automatic screw machine.[239] In Robbins' opinion, Waltham's advantage lay in its people and systems; he openly told shareholders that competitors could not match Waltham even if he displayed Waltham's tools and processes in their entirety.[240]

The days leading up to the opening of the Centennial Exhibition on May 10th were chaotic inside the Exhibition halls where companies and countries were to have set up their exhibits. Still, most failed to do so. By the opening morning, there were still thousands of tons of exhibits that had not yet arrived or been set up. Even a week after the opening, many displays by foreign countries were incomplete.[241] Swiss judge Edouard Favre-Perret remarked that "at the time of the opening of the exhibition it was very far from being ready with regard to the countries far away from the United States, and up to the end of July parcels still arrived which were admitted, but not without some difficulty."[242]

Waltham was the exception to the chaos. It sent a construction team and its exhibits to Philadelphia four weeks before the Centennial's inauguration. Like a well-planned military operation, the Waltham exhibit was set up a week before the opening. All eighteen Waltham employees that would operate the machinery at the Centennial arrived in Philadelphia around May 7th, three days before the massive Corliss steam engine brought the mini assembly line to life.

Even Charles Vander Woerd, the inventor of the automatic screw machine and the superintendent of the Waltham factory, "who certainly must be anxious that everything should be in proper condition," arrived days early with both his wife and daughter, reported the local newspaper.[243] While most companies and countries were mediocre in their level of planning and subsequent installation, Waltham showed a disciplined and creative company that strongly valued its potential at the Centennial both in the way it spent its time, money, and focus of company executives in the months and days leading up to the event.

The Waltham exhibit in Machinery Hall 1876 (Centennial Photographic Company, Public Domain)

In addition to its assembly line exhibit in Machinery Hall, Waltham had a second exhibit located in the American section of the Main Building. It occupied a small plot compared to the 21.5 acres that the building enclosed.[244] The exhibit was modest in size and garnered much less attention when compared to the assembly line exhibit. Still, it was grandiose in its message of industrial dominance, reading: "2200 watches representing six days work of 10 hours of the Waltham Watch Factory."[245] The display case was made with a dark, rich ebony wood, covered with plate glass showing off watches in ornamented gold and silver cases. The 2,200 watches represented a feat that would have taken a month or longer for an equivalent number of Swiss watchmakers to produce. It was a symbol of old-world art supplanted by new-world technology.

Impact of the Centennial on the Swiss

Waltham's two exhibits elicited the exact emotions for which Robbins had hoped. The Swiss were alarmed by what they saw. Swiss judge Favre-Perret reported that Waltham and other American watch companies: "deployed all their energy, and know-how, and employed all possible means to attract the eyes and the spirit of the visitors. All were implemented: not only one colossal exhibition but extensive advertising and numerous publications, widespread and profuse."[246] While he grouped American companies in his description, Waltham's exhibit was much more advanced and extensive than any other watch company, making Waltham his undoubted frame of reference.

What struck Favre-Perret most saliently was Waltham's well-planned and very dominant exhibit in the Main Building. He was alarmed and impressed by the "enormous display containing, as indicated by the following inscription with which it [was] decorated: '2200 gold and silver watches…'" He concluded this was simply impossible by any watchmaker in Europe.[247]

Waltham's preparation showed a marked contrast to its competitors including Elgin who also had a display case in the Main Building. Its exhibit consisted of a Victorian gothic-style stand with four small display cases showing a total sampling of about 200 watches. In addition, Elgin displayed some of its watchmaking tools elsewhere in the Main Building.[248] While Elgin was a production competitor to Waltham, it did not have the foresight to use the Centennial to capture the world's imagination. Elgin's participation mirrored the Swiss watchmakers more closely than Waltham's.

Nor did the Swiss watchmakers have the vision to see the Centennial as Robbins saw it. According to letters from the Swiss to the Centennial Commission, most of the producers did not "have a strong purpose to be represented at the exhibition," with the official Swiss representatives noting, "there seems to be but a languid interest felt through the country generally in the exhibition. [Swiss] Exhibitors are slow in representing themselves."[249] Much of this lethargy was due to the high tariffs on Swiss products, resulting in a general distaste for the American celebration.[250]

As 1876 approached, the Swiss merchants and producers started to accept the necessity of participation. Even as late as September 1875, while Waltham was undoubtedly already planning its exhibit, the Swiss delegation wrote that many Swiss firms still considered "an exhibition at Philadelphia as of no use whatever."[251] However, an attempt was made to have a modest presence at the Centennial, but the Swiss exhibit was a much smaller and limited display than shown in Vienna three years earlier and a marked difference from the 1851 Crystal Palace Exhibition where the Swiss watchmakers were an important object of pride and captured international fame.[252]

The resulting Swiss exhibit was attractive, but one account described it as "unenclosed, and is one of the plainest in the [Main] building in ornamentation."[253] The individual Swiss watchmakers each submitted a watch or two for display in an at-large display case in the Swiss section.

While innovation was displayed in other portions of the Swiss area, no new significant watch technology made it into the exhibit. The watchmakers' post-facto report complained that the Centennial Exhibition occurred only three years after the Vienna world's fair, which was too soon to "announce new discoveries."[254] This attitude demonstrated a divergence from Waltham, who regularly introduced noteworthy technological improvements, including its automatic screw machine.

As a metaphorical focal point of the Swiss exhibit was an electric clock manufactured and regulated by Mathias Hipp, who invented a novel way to adjust time across many clocks through the telegraph wire.[255] The Swiss were proud of his work with one prominent Swiss delegation member recounting, "we see with pride [the clock] industry replaced in our land by that of the electric clock, of which Mr. Hipp, of Neuchâtel, has indisputably the most vibrant and interesting display."[256]

An electric clock should have been a symbol of technological advancement in timekeeping with the ability to sync clocks across long distances. This would eventually enable standard time, having much more impact than Waltham's watches.[257] Yet it was Waltham's exhibit at the Centennial that was a reminder that it was the Swiss watchmakers who found their traditional art disappearing as a relic in the shadow of Waltham's advanced machinery.

As in watchmaking itself, the Centennial Exhibition was a clash between old and new world progress; a divergence of art and science.[258] Favre-Perret wrote: "Up to this very day we have believed America to be dependent upon Europe [for watches]. We have been mistaken."[259]

While the Swiss were alarmed, they were also frighteningly inspired. Rather than scaring the Swiss out of the market, the well-planned Waltham exhibit scared the Swiss towards action. Robbins thought the Centennial would seal the fate of foreign competitors and spur an insatiable demand for Waltham products. He was half correct. The Centennial brought Waltham international recognition and future sales. Yet, it also motivated the Swiss in an unforeseen way.

Chapter 6:

Mr. W.

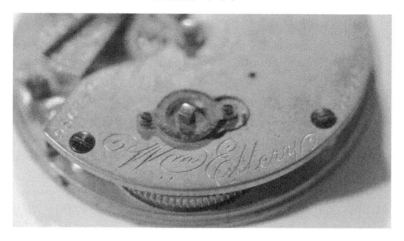

Waltham Ellery grade watch circa 1877 (Author's photo)

Centennial Exhibition – August 1876

Judging the best watches in the world

Judging products at the Centennial began almost immediately after the Exhibition opened and continued throughout the summer. Overseeing the evaluation of watches was the responsibility of Professor James Watson of the University of Michigan, and Edouard Favre-Perret, a respected Swiss watchmaker.

Watson and Favre-Perret supervised a group of eleven judges consisting of six Americans and five others representing the international. As the judges overseeing precision instruments, which included the brand-new telephone, they were, perhaps, the first to publicly endorse Alexander Graham Bell's novel invention. Watson would later recall: "In the performance of my official duty I took part in the experiments which first brought the speaking telephone to the notice of the scientific world ...Prof. [Alexander Graham] Bell had made a wonderful discovery, and that its complete development would follow in the near future."[260]

It did not take long for the judges to recognize Waltham's preparations. Measuring the excellence of Waltham's watches against the global competition meant they had to be tested using a standard performance metric. This was done by calculating a watch's accuracy compared to astronomical movements, which was done in an observatory. The Swiss had been doing this for their best watches for decades.

The finest Swiss watches were tested for accuracy at the astronomical observatories at Neuchâtel, built in 1857 in western Switzerland or the one in Geneva, built in 1829. The Swiss government sponsored contests through the observatories that contributed to manufacturing the best and most precise watches.[261] Professor Watson wrote, "Nothing has done more to stimulate the Swiss manufacture toward excellent workmanship and the most careful adjustments possible, than the competitive trials which have been made for a series of years at the Observatories at Neuchâtel and Geneva."[262]

The U.S. Government's national exhibit at the Centennial contained an observatory, allowing Watson and Favre-Perret to properly test the watches' accuracy. This task was handed over to Theo Gribi, whose "services as a mechanical expert were of great value."[263] In June, Gribi was given ten Waltham *AWC* grade watches to test, which were the company's best timepieces. Gribi's tests, along with seeing the assembly line exhibit, inspired him to write back to Switzerland with alarm, testifying that the Swiss had been overwhelmed by the American competition.[264]

Gribi had reason to be concerned. Not only had he witnessed Waltham's exhibit of small machines, but he also had a chance to experience the quality of its watches as a judge. In the final testing results, he determined that at least three Waltham watches were "altogether superior to any others exhibited," whether Swiss or American.[265] This allowed Waltham to claim that it made the best and most precise watches in the world. His tests "were sufficient to show that [Waltham's] claim of the production of first-class pocket chronometers was well founded."[266]

At the Centennial's awards ceremony, Waltham had little competition in the eyes of the judges. Nothing the Swiss put forward came close to equaling the ingenuity of Robbins' assembly line. One of the awards the company won was for "A System of Watchmaking."[267] According to the judges, Waltham's genius lay in "originality, as being the first to adapt the system of assembling interchangeable parts to the manufacture of watches."[268] As a physical token, Waltham received the standard 4" bronze medal awarded to all victors. The medal was only a symbol of a much greater prize. The true reward lay in capturing global markets and further diminishing the prestige of the most-celebrated Swiss watchmakers by marketing the results of the Centennial across the world.

Meeting Mr W

David and Gribi's mission to gather information about the American watch industry was a monumental task. The Centennial itself presented an obstacle for information collection. Waltham's machines were interesting but also limited in what they displayed. The Centennial judges noted in their report that "the machines gave some idea of the nicety, novelty, and ingenuity of the mechanism employed but could give but little impression of the variety and number of the machines in the factory."[269] Additionally, the official Centennial rules, which remained in place throughout the Exhibition, prohibited "Sketches, drawings, photographs or other reproductions of articles exhibited" and would "only be allowed upon the joint assent of the exhibitor and the Director-General."[270]

While David would eventually acquire very detailed sketches of equipment and manufacturing techniques, they were not acquired at the Centennial. Nor were most of the machines he lionized in his final report displayed by Waltham at the fair. Many of the machines he sketched and described were contained only inside company factories.

Most importantly, David and Gribi needed to learn how Waltham operated. It was obvious that machines were not the source of Waltham's advantage since most companies used similar designs. Additionally, Edward Bally, the vocal Swiss shoe factory owner, would have told David and Gribi about the futility of simply copying American machines. Bally's American machines had done him no good when competing with American factories. Waltham's machines were ingenious, but they alone were not the source of Waltham's competitive advantage.

David and Gribi needed to understand Waltham's culture, managerial systems, and the synergies that made it an innovative leader. Despite there being enough present at the Centennial to raise the alarm in Swiss watchmaking circles, the exhibits offered little help. David and Gribi could not complete their survey of American watch companies by simply acting as tourists wandering the grounds of Fairmount Park. They needed something more.

It was at the Centennial Exhibition that they probably first met Ambrose Webster. There is no record of the initial meeting or circumstances under which Webster became acquainted with David and Gribi, but the Centennial was almost certainly where it happened. Webster was the primary individual responsible for Waltham's award-winning watchmaking system. He retired from Waltham in June 1876 as Waltham's assistant superintendent and father of the company's interchangeable parts system. His department served as the beating heart of Waltham's vertically integrated model and was responsible for fabricating the machines used by the workers to make the watches.

Beginning in 1857, he oversaw the machine shop and supervised only a few workers. By the time of the Centennial, the shop would grow to about 50 machinists or 6% of the entire Waltham workforce and was one of the largest single departments in the watchmaking factory.[271] By the 1870s, he was appointed assistant superintendent, making him the third-highest company officer behind the superintendent Charles Vander Woerd and Royal Robbins.

In his retirement, Webster went to the Centennial Exhibition as a tourist.[272] There was no grander place to observe the latest innovations in machinery than the palace of industry. He could witness hydraulic rams, steam pumps, elevators, piston engines, fire extinguishers, circular saws, and lathes, whose creators all exhibited novel developments in machine tool technology.[273] Even some of Webster's inventions were in use at the Waltham exhibit. Eliza Putnam was operating his Webster/Marsh Automatic Pinion Machine before astonished visitors. Visiting Machinery Hall would have been a validation of his skill and also an intellectual playground for an accomplished machinist and inventor.

Webster may have even gone to the Centennial to find old-world watchmakers like David and Gribi, intent to shop his services.[274] Employees of companies frequently left to find new work, full of design secrets that regularly passed with veteran workers from firm to firm.[275] Waltham's machinists were especially in demand, with most of the American watch industry using derivations of Waltham's machine designs. The lack of effective design protection created an opportunity for Webster. If the Swiss could be convinced to transition to automatic machinery, he would have a chance at a lucrative second career by bringing Waltham designs to Switzerland.

David would write back to Switzerland in September 1876: "I cannot recommend wholeheartedly that W. [Webster] be engaged by a group of manufacturers or by one company, but I still believe this man will be a great help in any reorganization measures that we decide to implement."[276]

Or perhaps it was David and Gribi who realized that Webster had a set of skills and knowledge that the Swiss needed. Regardless of how it occurred, their meeting would change the course of the global watch industry for centuries to come.

Chapter 7:
An Unwelcome Guest

Waltham factory in the late 19ᵗʰ century around the time it was visited by David (Digital Commonwealth, Public Domain)

"Industrial espionage is the theft of information, more precisely the theft of trade secrets, something the holder wants to retain as a secret that is, proprietary information."

-Ilias Kaperonis, *Industrial Espionage*

Waltham Factory – September 1876

What is perhaps most ironic about the Waltham Watch Company's namesake town of Waltham is its claim to be the original home to one of America's most significant industrial heists in history: the textile mills founded by Francis Cabot Lowell.[277] In 1813, Lowell founded the Boston Manufacturing Company in Waltham, which at that time, was a small rural town about thirteen miles outside Boston. Lowell started his company using stolen proprietary information he had acquired through espionage.

Lowell knew the British had invented ways to vastly improve the efficiency of textile production. Their methods of production were so proprietary that a Harvard Business School case study notes that "companies went to great lengths to avoid information leaks, including closing mills to visitors, forcing employees to take secrecy oaths, designing factories 'with the defensive features of a medieval castle,' and even embellishing machinery to make it appear more complex."[278] According to Britain's Act of 1719, it was illegal to take skilled English workmen outside the country. A series of laws passed in the later eighteenth century expressly forbid artisans of wool and cotton as well as their designs and technology from leaving the country.[279] The law forbade Lowell from visiting the textile mill in Scotland, but the owner disregarded this as he viewed Lowell as too dumb to use what he saw.[280]

When he established the Boston Manufacturing Company, Lowell did not seek to *imitate* what he had seen at the British mills, rather, he realized that he could adapt the technology to take advantage of America's differences in culture, population, and geography. In 1813, Lowell improved British designs to make a more efficient system. Accordingly, he brought multiple stages of production under one large roof and established a factory in rural Waltham along the Charles River.

Lowell built a massive factory that employed 300 workers and consumed hundreds of thousands of dollars in capital in its first years of operation. All of these were marked contrasts to the British mills which separated stages of production in smaller urban factories using less-efficient machine designs. Lowell's final 'innovation' was developing idealistic working and living conditions to attract workers to the then-backwater town of Waltham. In contrast, the British factories operated under the guise of urban populations being willing to work in crowded squalor to survive.[281]

The terms 'emulate' and 'imitate' are often used interchangeably in the common lexicon, but they carry distinct differences in meaning. Imitate implies that one copies something exactly in action, trying to achieve the same outcome.[282] Emulation focuses less on the process and more on the result; it draws on the process to take hints and clues for developing a methodology but ultimately uses a unique approach to arrive at a similar or equal outcome.[283]

Because of Lowell's ingenuity and ability to comprehend ways to adapt the existing English systems, it resulted in emulation. He found that *emulation* allowed him to accomplish the same idea that the British had pioneered while adding his own superior innovation in its method and outcome. He was able to develop an entire system of manufacturing that would change the way America was able to compete in the quickly expanding global economy. His work became known as the Lowell-Waltham System for its uniqueness even though it relied directly on knowledge gained through espionage.[284]

David goes to Waltham

While the town had benefitted from espionage, it was about to be a victim. What started off as a fact-finding mission by David and Gribi at the Centennial

Exhibition quickly led to full-scale industrial espionage inside the Waltham Watch Company. David was the one primarily responsible for gathering information. Unlike Gribi who represented Swiss watchmakers at the world's fair as a judge, David was dispatched to conduct a "detailed survey" of American watch companies.[285] In the brief three months he spent in America, he documented few of his collection methods. But he did despairingly admit that in the days leading up to September 20th: "I sped through [the Waltham factory] quickly and incognito and saw the poor arrangements that I already knew about."[286]

One might wonder why David needed to sneak into Waltham's factory when he would eventually have multiple human sources, admitting in the same letter: "we have inside sources and we shall soon have the information we want".[287] Or why did he care so much about Waltham if many companies used machinery similar to Waltham's, including the large factory at Elgin?

David also had a considerable interest in Elgin, and many comparisons in his report would document procedures at both factories. However, the fact remained that David would spend more of his report focusing on Waltham, where it becomes evident to the reader that David could obtain more information from Waltham than anywhere else. In his writing, David would exclusively document the wages, cost structure, stock dividends, and production statistics from Waltham.

Additionally, David correctly identified Waltham as the market leader in reputation and production capability: he estimated that Waltham could produce 360 watches per day while Elgin could only make 260 per day. The next closest competitor had nowhere near that capability, only producing 85 watches per day.[288] It was Waltham that had won so many awards at the Centennial and was the focus of tourists and correspondents alike. Learning from Waltham was learning from the best.

Seeing the factory in operation was critical; simply learning about watchmaking machines did little good as the machine technology would quickly improve anyway. Stealing plans for the current models would never allow the Swiss to surpass the market leader. Therefore, David appeared to care much more about *how* Waltham operated rather than *what* it operated. The underpinning of Waltham's success was not the machines, but rather the management that created a culture of innovation, allowing it to scale its production faster than its competitors. David understood that he needed to learn about Waltham's systems and understand its culture, incentive structures, and managerial processes before he could ever surmise why the company was so successful in its sales and performance. Thus, Waltham became David's primary focus.

Entering the factory

After arriving in Waltham, David approached the factory on Crescent Street, the dusty yet manicured road that paralleled the Charles River.[289] Access to Waltham's factory was relatively secure, although more for the efficiency of profits than for security or safeguarding.[290]

Probably entering as a typical worker, he had to ensure he was inside before the company locked the

101

gates at the beginning of the workday, which occurred precisely at 7 AM.[291] Workers were tracked as they arrived and departed, which only happened in the morning, at lunch, and in the evening. David would note: "The purpose of this system is not only to obtain well organised work and to make too frequent absences known, which would be the cause of irregularity in such an employee, but it is also to determine exactly what the work costs."[292]

Historian Peter Stearns noted that employees during the industrial revolution had to "arrive when the factory whistle blew; if they were late, they would be locked out, lose half a day's pay, and be fined as much in addition."[293] This might have seemed oppressive compared to the more relaxed conditions in Switzerland, but drawing attention was something David could not afford.

Fortunately, a thick mustache and fit frame gave him a striking resemblance to the ordinary Waltham worker, many of whom looked as if they had been cut from the same mold. His French dialect was of little consequence as French Canadians were common in industrial New England and some Waltham workers were immigrants from Switzerland and myriad other places, settling in Boston.[294]

Waltham operated using an antecedent to scientific management. Foremen time-costed precisely every input that went into each part so the management could know exactly the cost of production down to each piece.[295] As David moved throughout the factory, he observed the strict discipline and tracking of workers. He noted: "Absences from each workshop are constantly controlled by the foreman or his assistant, and each workman who has to leave must ask permission."[296] What was impressive to David, but also inconvenient and an immediate danger if he was to avoid detection was the order, tempo, and rhythm of the work in each department. David noted: "They do not go from one workshop to another, they do not talk loudly, and the greatest courtesy reigns in the relationships between all personnel. The observation of these simple details facilitates the work of everyone."[297]

David was surprised when he found few signs of indiscipline or employee distractions. No workers smoked, drank alcohol, or meandered around the workshops; talking was kept to a minimum and any melodies of song or whistle were hardly audible. These were all marked contrasts to the working conditions common in Switzerland at the time.[298]

The only noises to be heard were those of the long, circular leather belts that rhythmically drove the machines, dropping from the ceiling to each worker's station. The noises were accented by a cacophony of grinding metal tools on metal parts. There was no yelling, no oppression by the foremen. The workers appeared to be treated with respect.[299] John Swinton, visiting eleven years later, noted that there was "no sign of subservience or slavishness, which as one is apt to look for in a factory. They are respected and self-respecting men and women, shrewd, intelligent, and of excellent demeanor."[300]

David's visit would be inexplicably short. He later recalled: "I did not really have time to have a good look around nor to ask questions."[301] Yet still, he observed particulars that only a keen observer would note, such as personal pictures hanging on the walls between stations.[302] In his report, he would write about American watch factories: "In all the workshops the

103

most rigorous cleanliness is maintained, and this care is encouraged by the pretty pieces of furniture, the offices, the lighting, and the very appearance of the benches which furnish the rooms. Some workshops are decorated with curtains, paintings, photographs of the workers, flowers, etc., which make being there very pleasant."[303]

The visit confirmed what others had told him. It further elevated his concern about the capabilities of Waltham and the future survival of the Swiss watch industry. He wrote with bewilderment: "Waltham greatly exceeds everything we have been told and everything we believed."[304]

He took solace in the fact that he had recruited many informants: "we have inside sources and we shall soon have the information we want."[305] His intelligence would come from "employees, the workmen in particular, and finally from discussions outside the factories with well-informed people."[306] They would be able to provide much more data than he could ever discover on his own. However, the best information would come from Ambrose Webster.

Chapter 8:

Loose Lips Sink Ships

Inside the Waltham factory in the late 19ᵗʰ century (Digital Commonwealth, Public Domain)

"We have, moreover, to safeguard the interests of the people who provided us with information. Some are employed in the factories and their situation would be seriously compromised if an indiscretion occurred."

-Jacques David, 1877

Waltham Factory – September 1876

In 1876, industrial espionage was not out of the ordinary for the era, nor would people have known it by that name. The earliest published use of the term 'industrial espionage' appeared around the start of World War I. It did not gain mainstream usage until the 1960s.[307] Historically speaking, humans have sought proprietary secrets to reduce a competitor's advantage. The mysteries of silk and porcelain were some of the most famous targets of industrial espionage.[308] It continues to be a relevant threat to modern companies. Some business leaders attribute the decline in U.S. competitiveness in the 1970s through 1990s to losses resulting from espionage.[309]

Putting the pieces together

While David's visit has not typically been associated with espionage, the indicators and evidence are not far from the surface. Once one knows of David's admitted incognito visit to Waltham and begins to view the situation through the lens of espionage, many other historical documents and events begin to fall into place.

A Swiss history about the era penned in 1947 mentioned David's visit to America. The history recounted that "Jacques David started by visiting the exhibition. The section of the watch industry was a mine of information. Glad to show their most successful products, the Americans had brought their sumptuous machinery and had constructed model workshops."[310]

An element of this was true, but the Centennial's exhibits provided little material for David; they were certainly not a "mine of information." The history continued by saying: "Jacques David continued his investigations on the spot where these frightening emulators made hundreds and thousands of good watches."[311] This portion was also an exaggeration as only a few parts of a watch were made at Waltham's exhibit, but not full watches.

The most alluring statement was about the spurious portion of David's mission, which it referred to as the *second part*. The history recounted: "Also, we think, this second part of his program was more delicate than the first, especially as, inopportunely, [David's] arrival in the United States 'had been announced by great cries from everyone.' He was right about all the obstacles."[312] The history never specified which obstacles David faced, but they assuredly existed, and it was supposedly inconvenient that people knew who he was.

Many horology enthusiasts familiar with David's report assume he was invited to the Waltham factory as a curious friend and the company freely and ignorantly shared its secrets with him. This was not the case. Even the above-quoted history provides a hint of this fact. The history recalls that people knowing who he was created an obstacle for his mission.[313] His identity would not matter nor have created an obstacle if David had been graciously invited to the various factories to freely observe and transfer information.

It is also not clear who even noticed David's arrival. His name does not appear in American records except the arriving ship's manifest. Given that he was an engineer from a new, struggling company, the claimed celebrity status in America was unlikely. At this point, David's company was not famous and the average Swiss watchmaker would not have garnered specific attention. Overall, the quoted account was minimal but said enough to demonstrate that there was more to the story than meets the eye, and even the Swiss author, writing in 1947, demonstrates this.

Unlike Gribi, David had no official roles at the Centennial and his name appeared nowhere in the

Centennial's official records. But this does not imply he was idle; the dates of his visit and subsequent reports indicate he began his work quickly. David arrived in Philadelphia about the 26th of August; shortly thereafter he traveled to Waltham. By September 20th he had already visited three factories in the Boston area, including Waltham.[314] It was only on his trip to Waltham that he admitted traveling incognito for a visit to the factory.

David the spy

David was not unique in his desire to learn about Waltham. Collecting information about competitors happened regularly in the industrial era as employees transitioned from one company to another. Professor of business Andrew Crane notes that:

> All organizations collect and make use of some kind of information about their competitors and other organizations, whether through market scanning, industry profiling, or simply debriefing of managers recruited from competitors. Indeed, such intelligence gathering activities are very much a standard aspect of conventional market research and competitor benchmarking, and make for effective competitive behavior.[315]

However, a line exists between market research and espionage. A spy who is "asked to gain access under a pretext to the company premises, to locate a specific item of plant or machinery, to photograph or draw it, to describe it and so on, that I would look upon as being industrial espionage," wrote experienced industrial counter-spy Peter Heims.[316] His 1982 analysis of industrial espionage was written as if to describe David's actions exactly.

Before the digital era, industrial espionage techniques usually involved "collection methods consisting of classic agent recruitments, volunteers, surveillance, surreptitious entry, and specialized technical operations."[317] These were all techniques David would eventually use. Heims noted that the use of disguises is one of the primary tactics of the industrial spy: "to gain entry to factories, workshops or offices [the spy] may need the same sort of uniform, overalls or other clothing which would disarm suspicion."[318] According to Heims' experience, David's claim of gaining access to the factory incognito was more than plausible, noting that "the business of infiltration (gaining access to plant, offices and premises for the purpose of observation and the theft of information, in whatever form) is by no means as difficult as some might imagine. Access to premises whose security is supposedly strict is often laughably easy."[319]

David's actions have not been widely characterized as espionage due to the known fact that Waltham frequently offered tours of the factory at points throughout its history.[320] In 1887, Swinton documented his own tour where he reported seeing virtually the entire factory: "On my own account and by the desire of the courteous [Royal Robbins], I made a thorough observation of the whole factory and all its features, from the engine room, through the numerous departments."[321] Robbins held the view that there was "no greater discouragement" to new competitors "than by the free exhibition of the factory itself and of all it contains."[322]

Of his documented visits to American factories, it was only at Waltham that David, in his own words, "sped through quickly and incognito...[and] did not really have time to have a good look around nor to ask questions."[323] Therefore, it was possible that David also took a cordial tour of the Waltham factory at some point on the company's terms. If such a tour occurred, David never acknowledged it.

Nor did Robbins have a disregard for secrecy as his earlier quote might imply. Rather, his statement about the free exhibition was more figuratively boastful than an open invitation. In 1869, he told shareholders, "Our affairs I need hardly tell you are the subject of great curiosity on the part of our competitors; and the Company's interest and that of every stockholder are obviously that no correct information of any consequence shall be suffered to leak out."[324] This implied both a practice of secrecy and possibly the use of misinformation to baffle competitors. Robbins and the company's board of directors also demonstrated a sensible suspicion of visitors interested in the operations and design of Waltham's machinery, even when compared to their primary competitor, Elgin.

An English horologist visited both factories around 1869 and reported remarkably different experiences between the two factories. At Waltham, the visitor "was somewhat surprised to find the directors were not so anxious to have the merits and capabilities of their machinery tested by a practical horologist." They did partially relent and allow him to at least see the machines, although "somewhat reluctantly." Despite getting to see the machines, and much to his dismay, the visitor did not receive permission to "publish and explain the peculiarities of [Waltham's] machinery and method." He gleefully contrasted this experience to his next visit to Elgin, where he "was invited to inspect and criticize their machinery and its productions, and publish its merits abroad."[325]

How David gathered the information

David's techniques for gathering data went well beyond factory visits. Of greatest interest to David in his correspondence and again in his final report were Waltham's financial operations and unit costs of production. Getting this information required filling in intelligence gaps with human informants. Much of the evidence in his final report came from people involved with Waltham and was neither publicly available nor would the topics have been information David could acquire in casual conversation. In fact, in 1869, fully aware of the interest of competitors in Waltham's operations, Robbins reminded the stockholders that any financial or strategic information he reported "shall be considered as confidential statements, to be kept strictly to ourselves."[326] For an employee or stockholder to share detailed financial information, it required intent, total ignorance, or negligence.

David began recruiting people who worked in the factory and those who simply knew about its operations. These individuals created a network that allowed him to systematically piece together Waltham's processes and procedures. This has historically been a common method for collection in industrial espionage. As recently as 1996, the Canadian Security Intelligence Service warned: "The most frequently used collection method is the recruitment of someone who has access to information (employees, contractors, consultants, students, etc.)."[327] Waltham employees might not have realized they were being used by David until it was too late, with "accidental exposure, usually owing to employee negligence, ignorance or carelessness" being one of the leading causes of industrial espionage, even in the modern era.[328]

This method of industrial espionage is usually employed under the guise of 'market research' where seemingly innocuous questions are directed toward employees to learn about the company and its operations.[329] According to Heims, this usually includes: "finding out all you can of your competitors' plans, methods, production schedules, sales techniques, markets, resources, staff, salary scales, designs, work schedules, production sequences..." He noted that the collection of this detail requires a skilled operative.[330] The topics of interest that Heims listed fit David's report exactly.

At least some of David's human intelligence sources were fully complicit in their participation even while working at the factory. In his report, David indicated that he had some informants he hoped to continue working with beyond 1876 to gain further information once back in Switzerland. This would imply those informants were cognizant of their actions, participating either because of reward or some kind of leverage held by David. He was concerned about leaking the true identities of his informants to protect them against retribution. He wrote that all efforts should be made to "safeguard the interests of the people who provided us with information. Some are employed in the factories and their situation would be seriously compromised if an indiscretion occurred."[331] David was successful; all his informants remain unknown to this day, except one.[332]

David even acknowledged that the American watch companies did not want him to have the information:

> *The most exact information was obtained directly from visiting the factories, from discussions with employees, the workmen in particular, and finally from discussions outside the factories with well informed people. All these means are more or less in the hands of the companies which can take severe measures to prohibit visits to the factories and communication with workmen, which they will not fail to do as soon as they know that these visits and conversations were used to the profit of a Swiss investigation.*[333]

Piecing together Waltham's operations

None of David's lower-level sources would have had the fidelity of data needed to piece together Waltham's financial and managerial operations. This required an executive who knew the final production numbers, sales figures, wages, and expenses. The average employee and even foremen would not have known this information.

Ambrose Webster was a solution to this problem. He knew Waltham having worked there for nineteen years as one of the company's most senior employees. Webster became a key source for David's investigation. David wrote Francillon in the fall of 1876 noting that Webster was helping him discern the workings and financial operations of the Waltham factory. David surmised that as far as the company's finances were concerned, he had "tried to work out their outgoings without reaching a precise result. Mr W, the former director on the mechanical side who is helping us in this respect…"[334]

By this point, David was referring to Webster casually as Mr. W., a common shorthand practice in the era when two people were acquainted with the subject. Therefore, Francillon was already familiar with the meaning of this shorthand, implying David probably wrote about Webster on numerous occasions in the less-than-thirty days he was in America when he sent the letter. It is also possible Webster started working with Gribi *before* David even arrived in America based on the familiarity with which David refers to him.

Webster was the probable source of most of the proprietary information acquired by David, but assuredly not all of it. David said he had seen "A very detailed document concerning the production at Waltham during the last months of 1876," which included production statistics by model.[335] Additionally, David acquired a Waltham document that accounted for periods *after* he returned to Switzerland in November 1876, indicating somebody was sending information to David beyond his stay in America.[336] David had to have recruited at least one person with access to the production schedule, exports, and profit & loss information who worked at the company after Webster retired.

In his final report, David provided the following production numbers by month (in the table below), noting the approximate watches produced and their value. He cited seemingly precise data from the fall of 1876 and winter of 1877, provided by a source in the

114

company. As the figures show, they were very exact, and the averages indicate that he was not using simple average prices to arrive at the total value.

Month (1876-77)	Production	Value	Average Value
October	6500	$63,000	$9.69
November	8450	$85,390	$10.11
December	8200	$83,910	$10.23
January	7900	$78,800	$9.97
February	8600	$74,000	$8.60

Aggregate total numbers from David's final report. The averages have been added by the author. Note the exactness of the numbers, including the values reported by David. (Author's work, see David p. 81)

Given Waltham's relatively hierarchical structure, very few employees would have had access to this strategic-level information. This data was not even published to shareholders as it was only reported annually in an aggregated figure in the company's report that was verbally read and "not intended for general publication."[337] The monthly production data David cited were tracked inside the company's ledgers and on production documents, which were likely circulated amongst senior management. This indicated he still had contacts inside Waltham with access to this high-level production data as late as February 1877, who were sending it to him in Switzerland.

Webster could have been the source of this very specific and non-public information, but only if he was actively seeking it on David's behalf. Therefore, as David admitted, and his data showed, he had active contacts at all levels of the company when he published his final report. David stated that he hoped to remain in communication with his contacts: "we can hope to maintain the relationships which we have made and continue to be informed by people in close contact with the factories."[338] Given the currency of his data, it appears he was successful in his wish.

David acknowledged the difficulty of gaining general financial information, writing: "The watch factories, being mainly private companies, do not publish any reports and it is difficult to know exactly what dividends they pay."[339] An example of David's abnormal access to Waltham's private financial numbers was seen in his report about Waltham's profit and loss statement. David made the following estimates, which are compared below to Waltham's actual expenses as recorded in its surviving profit-and-loss ledgers maintained in the archives of Harvard Business School.[340]

Expense	David's Estimates	Actual Expenses
Salaried Employees*	$50,600	$48,220
Heating & Engine**	$4,500	$4,237
Insurance	$6,000	$1,646
Gas lighting	$3,500	Not Reported***
Building Repairs	$1,000	$1,978
Night guards, cleaning, transport	$5,000	Not Reported***
Materials****	$82,400	$78,739

*Includes 2x Superintendents, 3x Office workers, and all company foremen

**It is assumed David was referring to 'heating and engine' Oil. Oil is what Waltham's Profit and Loss statement notes

***Waltham's P&L statement did not report these line items. There was a line for fuel, in which gas could be included into or there was also a catch-all line called 'Expenses' within which these would likely be reported

****David reported materials under three separate lines, which I have combined as Waltham does not separate them. Because materials could be stockpiled, I have averaged the material costs of Waltham for 1876-1877

Source: Profit and Loss Statements, Waltham Records, Vol. C-1, Baker Library, HBS

David's estimates were remarkably accurate. He acknowledged: "We will give some figures which can only be approximate but which we can guarantee are sufficiently exact to be of interest."[341] The numbers demonstrated that he received information from someone with close knowledge of the company's financial operations, but they were not accurate enough to indicate David personally viewed the company's Profit and Loss statements.

David reported numbers on Waltham's employees and wages that were even more accurate. He said that "Absolute secrecy reigns between the workmen on the amount of their pay, and they appear to maintain this discretion."[342] David's report cited Waltham's estimated wages by job type. When using these to create a weighted average pay at Waltham, David's estimates equate to an average daily wage for all employees of $1.78.[343]

This demonstrates David's fidelity of information when comparing his estimate to Waltham's actual payrolls maintained in Harvard's archives. Daily wages for individual workers could range anywhere from less than a dollar to as high as five or six dollars.[344] Looking specifically at September 1876 Waltham's employees were paid an average wage of $1.77 per day, only $0.01 below David's estimate.[345] [346] Therefore, at least one of his informants had to know detailed information about Waltham's wages in totality. This aggregated wage information likely came from Webster, the former assistant superintendent.

Webster's role

No information on the enduring communications between Webster and David exists. However, much of what happened can be interpolated based on David's writings as well as a few specific but financially risky actions by Webster. Overall, David saw a future role for Webster in the Swiss recovery, and

117

Webster appears to have established himself to profit from a Swiss transition.

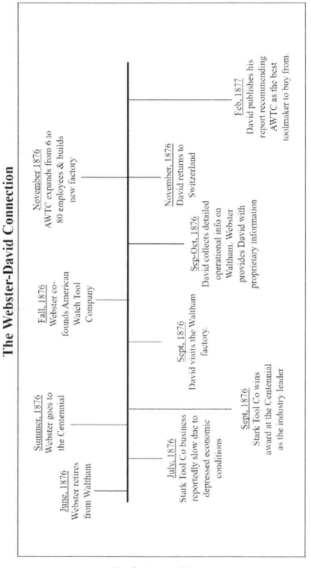

The Webster-David Connection

June, 1876 Webster retires from Waltham

July, 1876 Stark Tool Co business reportedly slow due to depressed economic conditions

Summer, 1876 Webster goes to the Centennial

Sept, 1876 Stark Tool Co wins award at the Centennial as the industry leader

Sept, 1876 David visits the Waltham factory.

Fall, 1876 Webster co-founds American Watch Tool Company

Sep-Oct, 1876 David collects detailed operational info on Waltham. Webster provides David with proprietary information

November, 1876 AWTC expands from 6 to 80 employees & builds new factory

November, 1876 David returns to Switzerland

Feb, 1877 David publishes his report recommending AWTC as the best toolmaker to buy from.

(Author's work)

118

Webster's second career began almost immediately upon his retirement from Waltham in June 1876. The *Waltham Free Press* noted, "Although [Ambrose Webster] has earned a long rest, yet we doubt if he is long content with inactivity." [347] The newspaper was correct; Webster joined and helped form the American Watch Tool Company (AWTC) in the fall of 1876.

He partnered with John E. Whitcomb, another machinist who left Waltham in 1872 and owned a company that made various mechanized equipment, including watchmaking machinery. The firm came with a good reputation but did not produce the best tools available. According to the judges of the Centennial Exhibition, that award went to John Stark's firm, also of Waltham, Massachusetts whose combination lathe and watchmaking tools were "commended for adaptability to different uses, and quality of workmanship and materials."[348]

Just four months after Webster joined the small firm of six employees, David recommended the AWTC to his Swiss counterparts, which he claimed was the best American producer of watchmaking tools. David did not even recommend Stark Tool Company as his second choice, rather he recommended George Hart of New Jersey.[349] In the fall of 1876, AWTC was in the process of a quick and vast expansion, but David's recommendation of Webster's newly formed company had to rely more on potential than anything else. AWTC's offering was relatively limited when compared with the Stark Tool Co.

It was in September 1876 that David wrote to Francillon to propose the idea of approaching Webster about involvement in the Swiss transformation.[350] Thus it was not coincidental that a large expansion of the AWTC occurred under Webster. When he joined the company in the fall of 1876, it had six employees. By November, the company announced plans to build a new factory and hire eighty workers.[351] In comparison, the well-established Stark Tool Co only employed fourteen workers and the local Waltham newspaper reported that Stark experienced slow sales and a large work-in-progress inventory due to the depressed economic conditions of 1876.[352] Similarly, during this same period, the Waltham Watch Company had furloughed most of its workforce for the summer as a result of the depressed economic conditions and only returned to full strength in October 1876 after a long partial shutdown. The other two watch companies David had visited in Massachusetts were also shut down in the fall of 1876 due to poor economic prospects.[353] Yet Webster's company invested in a new factory and grew the workforce by 1300% while the economy still suffered.

Webster's confidence in massive business growth opportunities was unusually high given the economic realities and the company's lower market position. Webster had to have believed in a forthcoming windfall of business opportunities both from the Swiss and other American and English watchmakers with whom he also began work after the Centennial. If the Swiss watchmakers transitioned to the Waltham model of production, AWTC would be well-positioned to meet the demand.

Overall, David's recommendation of Webster's company to the Swiss watchmakers provides probable evidence of a fulfilled arrangement. David's letter of September 1876 to Francillon indicated he was already considering this approach: "I cannot recommend wholeheartedly that W. [Webster] be engaged by a group of manufacturers or by one company, but I still believe this man will be a great help in any reorganization measures that we decide to implement."[354] While Webster was providing sensitive information to David, David was securing Webster's long-term involvement in the Swiss transformation through business opportunities. His recommendations of Webster almost certainly had nothing to do with the AWTC's reputation or performance at the time.

By 1892, it was said that Webster had visited almost every watch factory in Switzerland.[355] Evidence shows that Webster certainly helped David gain information about Waltham, while history demonstrates that Webster benefitted from the Swiss transformation, though evidence of an agreed arrangement is not confirmed.

There is no doubt that David completed one of the most covert and successful industrial heists in history. The question remained: even if the Swiss could match Waltham's production methods, could they match Waltham's systems and future innovation? Could the Swiss regain everything they had lost, overpowering Waltham in the global markets? If Edward Bally's Swiss shoe factory was any indication, the answer was no. As the Swiss had discovered, "the possession of the best machines of today is not enough to enable a country to sustain itself in industrial competition."[356] The Swiss could not simply replicate what they had seen, nor was there any indication that they could match Waltham's ingenuity. By the late fall of 1876, the Swiss watch industry appeared condemned.

Chapter 9:

Weapons Against Us

"...it was agreed that the discussion would not be published in journals, so as not to wake the indiscreet attention of [American] manufacturers and not to give them weapons against us by too openly making the truth [of their advantage] known to them."

-Jacques David, 1877

Centennial Exhibition – November 1876

A dark storm cloud gathered over Fairmount Park on a cold autumn day in November as thousands of visitors gathered outside the Judges' Hall to watch President Grant bring the Centennial Exhibition to a close. This marked the end of America's grandiose introduction to international markets and the world's imagination for invention.

In the opinion of the Centennial's historian James McCabe, Americans were previously "regarded as a smart half-cultured people, of immense energy and remarkable ingenuity, but deficient in the higher graces and achievements of civilization, and depending upon the Old World for all finer grades of manufactures."[357] Even the 'cultured' Europeans admitted that America had advanced itself. It seemed to be understood that America's successful showing at the Centennial would come with a consequence for the rest of the world, with Edward Bally writing: "Philadelphia has been, so to speak, the key by which American industry will unlock for itself the road to Europe and to its colonies."[358] The general opinion was that Americans had "discovered that many articles which we have been buying from other countries can be profitably made here and that many which we already make can be improved in quality or in the element of taste, or produced at lower cost, so as to command new markets."[359]

Waltham exploits its success

American companies took awards in every category, including the Waltham Watch Company in Group XXII. Swiss judge Edouard Favre-Perret had witnessed everything Waltham had to offer at the Centennial. He admitted that Waltham's "factory is a real power; there is none like it in Europe," and dishearteningly told the Swiss watchmakers: "I do not pretend to point out the remedy. I simply call your attention to the evil—that is all. It remains for you to find the cure."[360]

Waltham immediately began to exploit its success through an aggressive marketing campaign. It had made every effort to ensure its exhibits would capture the world's imagination and inform foreign competitors of Waltham's dominance. This was not lost on Favre-Perret who noted that "[Americans] have deployed all their energy, and know-how, and employed all possible means to attract the eyes and the spirit of the visitors."[361] He rhetorically questioned whether anything further was required by the American watch companies to "succeed in eclipsing and pushing into the background their European competitors? These companies…did not simply present "specimens" of what they can do, but rather veritable warehouses," particularly noting Waltham's display of 2,200 watches.[362]

Remarks like this of Favre-Perret showed that Robbins understood what separated Waltham and his Swiss competitors more than anything else was the perception of its reputation, particularly through advertising and word of mouth. David was amazed that the American watch companies had managed to maintain a positive reputation for consistency across such a broad spectrum of products produced.[363] This positive perception was deserved and well-cherished by Waltham. An example of this was shown after a fire at a small Waltham facility in 1877. Robbins reported to shareholders that many of the watches in the fire could probably be repaired, but "they will all therefore be broken up, so that dealers and the public, may rest assured that our name will not be used, to palm off an injured watch."[364]

There was no better testimony of Waltham's pristine reputation than the words of the Swiss judge Favre-Perret. Waltham used its marketing expertise to project the reputation it had earned at the Centennial while also exploiting Favre-Perret's own opinions about Waltham. The company widely published and advertised a speech Favre-Perret gave to Swiss watchmakers upon his return to Switzerland in November 1876. The speech was a report on the state of affairs in the watch industry that carried a distressing tone. A widely-published excerpt from his speech read:

> *Here is what I have seen, gentlemen! I asked from the director of the Waltham Company a watch of the [lower quality]. A large safe was opened before me; at random I took a watch out of it and fastened it to my chain. [Later I]*

handed the watch to [a watch] adjuster, who took it [apart]...he came to me and said, word for word, 'I am completely overwhelmed; the result is incredible; one would not find one such a watch among fifty thousand of our [Swiss] manufacture.'[365]

Waltham seized on Favre-Perret's words in a brilliant marketing performance. It published the speech as an appendix to Professor Watson's final report from the Centennial, which explained Waltham's exhibits in detail.

Favre-Perret's speech captured the tenor of the Centennial in the eyes of most Americans and was the embodiment of the effect Waltham hoped to have: the Swiss were alarmed and could not compete with American ingenuity. The publication was a summary of Waltham's performance in global competition, followed by the lead Swiss judge admitting that Waltham was in the process of conquering the Swiss watch industry. The publication could be obtained by anyone in America, free of charge by requesting a copy through the mail. The free report's availability was advertised by Waltham in newspapers across the country.

Excerpts of and summaries from Favre-Perret's speech also appeared in newspapers nationwide. The frequency of articles mentioning Favre-Perret emphasized the importance of the watch industry to the global economy of that time. These articles reported everything from the despair of the Swiss to reports that the Swiss had abandoned further construction of a watchmaking school.

Newspapers created an image of a Swiss industry forsaking the watch trade. According to the

126

American press, the famed Swiss judge "has not only no hope of [a Swiss-American watch trade] recovery, but looks forward to the time when it shall be lost altogether."[366] Another newspaper reported that a commission was introduced in Switzerland to "inquire what industry could be introduced in place of that which must henceforth be abandoned to American competitors."[367]

In the eyes of the American press, Favre-Perret's words proved American dominance, playing directly into the nationalistic feelings of the era. In the month following the Centennial, a Chicago newspaper wrote that "A man is almost ashamed in these days to be found carrying anything but an American watch."[368] Another newspaper noted that American watches were "destined to muster the entire field."[369]

Robbins reported Waltham's success to shareholders: "The fact has at last come out, and is freely admitted in the foreign producing districts, that our system is the only true one, and our factory the best existing illustration of that system. Our triumph at Philadelphia was *undoubtedly the most conspicuous of all American successes.*" (Author's emphasis).[370]

Both Americans and even the British believed that the Swiss watchmakers were doomed in the face of technological progress of the machine and factory. The newspapers wrote unapologetically: "we are sorry for the crisis, but in economics such is the rule of the game."[371] The Swiss simply could not match American capital, or so people thought, with the widely circulated *Chambers's Journal*, a British publication, writing: "Skill, capital, and machinery are sure to carry the day. In the progress of affairs, the old must give place to the new."[372] It suggested that "In such cases the best plan is not to maintain a useless struggle."

The magazine offered one piece of advice that would prove prescient in the face of the Swiss watchmakers' demise. It recommended the Swiss "go over to the enemy – try to rival him on his own ground...the only thing the Swiss can do is to adopt the same species of machinery into their manufacture."[373]

The journal was right. In the opinions of the members of the Swiss delegation to the Centennial, they had seen incontrovertible evidence that the Swiss watch industry would quickly be extinguished in the absence of a coherent change to the way the industry operated. Jacques David, operating in the shadows of the Centennial, warned his fellow watchmakers:

> "All will be lost. The same situation occurred in other industries. For a long time [those industries] exported products to the United States until indigenous manufacture developed and made this exportation impossible. What has occurred in the [Swiss] manufacture of machinery, leathers, cottons, cloths and the silk trade will happen in the watch industry."[374]

David's report

David returned to Switzerland in November 1876. He worked on his report, which would eventually encompass 130 pages of detailed drawings and descriptions. His report would not be an encyclopedia of machines, but rather a comprehensive analysis of financial, production, and operating procedures including everything from machine and factory designs, to how the management dealt with the pay of workers. It primarily focused on Waltham and noted many details from Elgin and other American watch companies. The report would be finalized by January 1877 and presented to the watchmakers' trade union at Neuchâtel, deep in the Jura mountains.[375]

David's work was one report of at least a few written by other delegation members that called for the Swiss to move from their cottage industry system towards the factory. There was also Favre-Perret's speech that was widely circulated, and then his subsequent written report. As early as November 1876, Favre-Perret wrote: "Had the Philadelphia Exhibition taken place five years later we should have been totally annihilated without knowing whence or how we received the terrible blow. We have believed ourselves masters of the situation, when we really have been on a volcano." [376]

Favre-Perret's short report and speech would have served as the initial emotional shock for those Swiss watchmakers who were willing to listen. David's report followed a few weeks later with immense detail and confirmation of everything Favre-Perret had said. David's report offered recommendations that were both radical and, eventually, his ideas would prove to have an outsized influence on the Swiss and their transformation towards the factory.

The first significant element of David's report was the attention it drew to the problem the Swiss were facing by confirming everything being reported by other members of the Swiss delegation to the Centennial Exhibition. While some Swiss watchmakers saw a dire future, most saw no immediate threat at all, with most of the watchmaking community not believing there was clear evidence of a problem. Many of the resistant watchmakers acted similarly to former Microsoft CEO Steve Ballmer, who admittedly laughed when he first saw the iPhone, refusing to believe that it could ever be a viable threat. David joined others in insisting on the immediacy of the threat despite a languid reaction by most.

One aspect that set David's report apart, seen from the opening paragraphs to the conclusions, was his optimism for change among the radical recommendations he would make for transforming the Swiss watchmaking system. David opened his report by saying: "Unfortunately we can only confirm everything said by Mr. Favre-Perret; competition is very vigorous and very skilfully organized; it is high time we made serious efforts if we are not to lose more ground and be completely supplanted within a short time, by this industry which has existed for only a few years and which is already powerful and sophisticated."[377]

The second significant element of David's report was its thorough analysis of the machinery, operations, and financial conditions of Waltham and Elgin. In detail, David described Waltham, noting conditions such as: "The tools at Waltham are valued at $400,000 and would, we were assured, cost as much to make now. The expenditure on their construction was vastly higher than this figure. It is estimated that the grounds and buildings cost $300,000. The total capital of the factory is $1,800,000."[378]

David's description of the tools provided an even more detailed analysis: "Another characteristic of the American machines is the perfect construction of the clamps and other tools used to hold the parts being manufactured. These clamps, called chucks are of various designs according to the use for which they are intended. The simplest and most widespread is a small cylindrical support finished with a conical head..."[379]

This level of detail was a marked divergence from the other prominent Swiss reports such as those by Favre-Perret which only provided a higher-level perspective of the problem. The limits of Favre-Perret's recommendations were captured in statements such as this: "We do not consider the situation which we are in to be irremediable; far from it. Without too much difficulty we can adapt the machines and progress which has been made in the United States in the field of horology."[380] Most of his broad strokes were neither that insightful nor actionable.

Swiss skepticism

David's report called for collective action. It was not a motivational speech, but rather a detailed plan that insisted on discrete steps that could be made by individuals, the government, and the collective body of watchmakers. David identified the predicament as "extremely serious and that it will continue to worsen if we do not act vigorously."[381] David saw emulation of American factories as the only prudent response if watchmaking were to survive as an industry in Switzerland. He wrote:

> An exact copy of what America has done is not what we recommend. We do not demand that all workmen are united under the one roof, nor that we manufacture ebauches [base or parts of a watch movement], assortments, balances, dials, hands, springs, etc. under only one management. We only recommend

that we take particular features of these factories, like the system of manufacture, and that we apply them as well as possible to Swiss manufacture.[382]

The initial skepticism David faced was ingrained in the watchmaking culture, which saw no need for factories. Francillon even validated this notion earlier in 1876 when he wrote: "We cannot think of setting up in our mountains powerful companies having millions of dollars and thousands of workmen. It neither suits our customs nor our interests. But what we can do is to syndicate with a common aim."[383] Factories had already found their way to businesses such as Bally's shoe industry and factories were well known in firearms and textile manufacturing. In David's view, watchmaking in a factory was a natural future progression.[384]

Much of the opposition to factories in Switzerland stemmed from centuries of economic patterns where Swiss farmers used watchmaking to make additional money, which they could quickly put back into their land.[385] Asking them to work in factories ran counter to their lifestyle and infringed on individual independence as a proprietor, which was the primary goal for most. Many Swiss farmers' entire fortunes were in their land and livestock, yet a factory required concentrating workers in a small geographic area, usually a large city, something that was not conducive to farmers who lived and worked large swaths of land and were unaccustomed to city life. Unsurprisingly, few Swiss watchmakers energetically embraced David's suggestion of the factory concept.[386]

Some of the Swiss even assumed the perspective of the Luddites of England that destroyed textile machinery, fearing that introducing technology would surely eliminate jobs. An English article entitled 'The Effects of Machinery on Wages' skeptically noted: "If the Swiss employers introduce machinery and the demand for their watches remains as it is, they could afford employment [of] only 8,400 persons instead of 40,000 as at present."[387] People assumed that efficient machinery meant fewer workers were required. In reality, the people at the greatest risk of losing their jobs to a machine were those few skilled master craftsmen since a machine was cheaper, more accurate, and carried no ego. David anticipated this obstacle and would account for the skilled artisans in his proposal.

David's vision for a hybrid factory system

Undoubtedly, the Swiss watchmakers benefited from David and Gribi's mission and the knowledge gained through espionage. They learned about Waltham's advanced machinery, designs, and strategies for the production of specific parts which informed the Swiss industry's transformation. David wrote: "In the United States, the most ingenious procedures were originally worked out by the mechanics who run the factories; *they are procedures without which, it is admitted, one cannot work practically.* These procedures...I described in detail in my report..." (author's emphasis).

David also suggested that the Swiss benefit "from the methods that our [American] competitors have discovered,"[388] but since David also cited Waltham as the company that originally worked out most of the mechanical solutions, the Swiss benefitted from the methods that Waltham pioneered.[389] The Swiss needed a factory system to take advantage of these advanced methods.

The system David envisioned did not require large factories, but rather organized syndicates of individual producers who each played a part in the larger manufacturing process. Waltham had many departments that each produced a piece of the final product, all under one roof. David's concept disaggregated this system from vertical integration into a decentralized model. He envisioned that each of Waltham's departments could become its own "factory," or in some cases, many small factories, staffed by existing watchmakers or parts makers.

For example, one group of Swiss watchmakers would form together and focus on making watch movements, another making cases, and even another finishing the watches. These groups of watchmakers would further divide the parts manufacturing to subcontracted factories or production groups that used standardized methods of measure and selective mechanized production to ensure uniformity. As such, the Swiss system would use a flatter integration of very small factories or workshops united by standard designs and systems of measurement.

Universal agreement on a few common models and sizes would allow decentralized production while maintaining an industry standard, allowing watch movements from one maker to be universally pairable with a watch case made by another without deliberate coordination. Adopting common specifications across the industry would seem intuitive, but it also asked the decentralized, independent watchmakers to give up an element of their individual creativity. This even included stipulating a common size and angle of threading for screws.[390]

134

Parts that required precision machining would be done in the larger factories. Everything else that did not require machine-level precision would be produced through subcontractor agreements, usually in people's homes or small local workshops.[391] In David's words: "If later we see some advantage in also making [more parts] in the [central] factory we will do it, but we believe that [many parts] can be made outside the factories as long as the suppliers agree to it, and that way we will find a great simplification in the initial organisation."[392]

Under David's proposal, once a mechanical movement was assembled and manufactured by a 'factory' and its syndicate of workers, it was expected to meet basic quality control requirements such as standardized parts, a guarantee of operation, and easy repair. David also specified that standardized movements should come with repair parts, which was a defense against Waltham's ease of repair and warranties.[393] The completed mechanical movements were then sold to the final manufacturers who were usually the brand name of the watch.[394] The final manufacturer was responsible for the fine adjustments of the timing, any decorative engraving, and final testing to ensure the watch worked correctly and met stringent industry standards.[395]

The system operated much like a modern computer manufacturer who gathers major components from suppliers; the supplier further gathers smaller components from sub-suppliers. The computer manufacturer assembles, tests, and cases the final product and is ultimately responsible for its performance. Many modern Swiss watch brands still purchase standardized watch movements and other parts from third-party manufacturers, while providing small customizations, adjustments, and finishing.

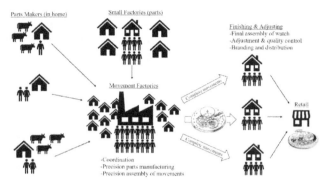

David's model to transition the Swiss to precision mass manufacturing using the existing cultural and geographic structure. (Author's work)

David's vision was palatable because it suggested that only the minimum number of production steps move to an American-style factory. This meant that few people had to drastically change their lifestyle or geographic location, ensuring cultural acceptance of the system. It allowed most parts-makers to continue their work without major environmental changes if they could maintain rigorous standards of precision. David concluded that this way of operation would provide a minimal viable industrial system.[396]

David's proposed system would also allow the coordinating, smaller factories to quickly shift to new trends in consumer preferences because they did not have expensive sunk costs in machinery that produced an antiquated model of watch. Changes in models were expensive for a single company like Waltham and required retooling an entire factory. Under the Swiss system, the coordinating factories could simply direct the subcontractors to make a change. This was relatively easy at the subcontractor level since few had complicated machines. Most of the parts production was still distributed to craftsmen, able to skillfully manipulate their machines.[397] Additionally, most of the Swiss machines that were eventually used were more versatile versions of American models. The machines required a more skilled operator but could also be adapted for variety with little or no switching costs.[398]

Resistance to David's report

Swiss resistance to acknowledging and acting to fix the problem seemed to come from all quadrants. Despite wide-spread knowledge of cratering Swiss watch sales, David found almost universal doubt of his findings and report. Even David's espionage partner Theo Gribi implicitly doubted that David's proposed plan could prompt a viable recovery of Swiss watchmaking.

After the Centennial Exhibition, Gribi quickly returned to America and married Sarah Week of Stevens Point, Wisconsin on January 1, 1877, a month before David even published his report. Gribi had met her while in Philadelphia for the Centennial. Additionally, when not courting Sarah Week, judging watches, or helping David probe American companies' operations, Gribi searched *for jobs* with American watch factories. During the Centennial, he "decided to make his services available to the leading [watch] factories and in the course of time suitable arrangements were made with several of the leading manufacturers."[399]

At the close of the Centennial, he accepted a job at Elgin and eventually took charge of its adjusting department. After seven years there, he took a position at Waltham in 1885.[400] By the end of his life, Gribi "played an important part in effecting certain refinements that have made possible the excellent performance of so many of our American-made watches."[401] In 1892, he also organized the American Horological Society where "he foresaw a society that would represent and advance the status and standing of the watchmakers of [America]." His peers elected him as its first president and is considered the father of professionally organized watchmakers in America (which still endures).[402]

As David's partner, having seen the same data, Gribi found America to be the future of watchmaking. Despite any positive words he might have said about a Swiss recovery, Gribi's quick departure implicitly sent the message that he had seen exactly what David had seen, but that David's proposed plan had little realistic chance of success.

The loudest public voices of dissent came from the famous Swiss watchmakers who were small-batch producers and had little reason to worry about sales as they still received orders. Luxury producers like A. Lange & Söhne,[403] Patek, Philippe, & Co, or Matile were powerful anomalies that hardly represented the status quo of the broader industry. Most Swiss watchmakers were unknown to the consumer except for their infamy as producers of shoddy products that collectively required millions of dollars annually to repair. These peasant watchmakers were entirely reliant on a future vibrant, reputable industry and found themselves captive to whatever fate came to the industry.

The stalwarts believed that watchmaking was an art that no automatic machinery could replicate. David saw evidence that proved them wrong, but they refused to back David's report, shedding doubt on its reliability, and also threatening the future of the entire regional economy. Many prominent watchmakers also attacked David's work as flattery towards American industry. In March, 1877, a full four months after the conclusion of the Centennial, David complained of an "almost complete quietude in a country which should be seeking by every means possible to shift its industry out of the rut in which it is stuck, and to cure it of an extremely serious disease which it has caught and whose symptoms are already too obvious."[404]

Convincing the industry to reorganize would require more than dire warnings, which is what made David's report unique as it offered a detailed plan of transformation that accounted for many unique aspects of the socio-economic spectrum of western Switzerland. David viewed collective action as the only plausible road to recovery. David saw strength in the Swiss' reliance on each other for economic survival:

> [this plan] can only have effect if [it is] adopted and supported by a great number of the interested parties. The association, or at least the union, of the vital forces in Swiss industry is absolutely necessary if we are to preserve in our country the industry which has for so long made us prosperous. This is why, in concluding, we fervently hope that this union is possible, and that we will soon see emerging, from the various centers of our industry, active relationships defending our interests against threats.[405]

Favre-Perret more eloquently and succinctly said the same: "And finally, let us put into practice our beautiful motto 'one for all, all for one.' Let us group our forces, and we will promptly and surely arrive at the resurgence of our beautiful industry. What others did we can do, and we will do."[406] Their approach of appealing to collective action was keen: each watchmaker relied on the production community as an economy of agglomeration.[407]

While radical in its suggestions, David's plan emphasized the importance of continued inter-reliance and response by the whole community. Low wages and few farming prospects made the Swiss unusually reliant on watchmaking for subsistence and they were willing to do almost anything to preserve their way of life.[408] A contemporary reporter remarked on the few options the Swiss watchmakers had:

> The Swiss will not surrender their American market without a renewed struggle...The principal advantage is the low rate of wages which must be accepted by men occupying the sterile valleys of the Jura, where agriculture is impossible, and where they have been from their childhood devoted to this one calling. They must make watches, if not for good wages, then for poor wages.[409]

Responding to change was a laudable attribute of the Swiss watchmaking community. The Swiss watchmakers had a history of adapting, improving on the methods of others and doing the job infinitely better than foreign competition. Economics professor Richard Langlois described the Swiss watchmakers as "hardly tradition-bound, welcoming new ideas so long as they promised a profit."[410]

Despite a history of change and collective action, one of the greatest obstacles that David's plan would have to overcome was the socio-economic structures. Many owners of small workshops were comfortable with their position in the existing market order despite pervasive poverty. Historian Pierre-Yves Donzé noted: "this economic conservatism was shared by numerous subcontractors, usually without any wealth, for whom the workshop was the only family asset. For them, [movement towards the proposed] industrialization meant the end of their autonomy and of their professional activities."[411]

In the shadows for 125 years

David's report would not result in a centrally coordinated effort to transform the entire Swiss watchmaking economy. Yet, David's report and its conclusions could be seen with surprising clarity throughout the forthcoming changes to western Switzerland over the next three decades. Coupled with the ardent reports of Favre-Perret and a few others, David's report would suggest most of the changes that eventually happened in Swiss watchmaking, including strategic choices and actions that would ultimately result in the Swiss recovery.[412]

Even through the wisdom of David's report and the forthcoming transformation of the watchmaking regions, he would not end up with much of the credit until recent decades. This was because David was concerned that his report would be used against the Swiss much like Favre-Perret's speech had been. David wrote: "It is thus of the first importance not to talk about the present investigation and to communicate this report only to reliable people who can extract from it portions useful for this country. In this manner we can hope to maintain the relationships which we have made and continue to be informed by people in close contact with the factories."[413]

For the sake of not providing Waltham with further advertising material and protecting David's informants in America, the watchmakers' trade union (SIIJ) limited distribution of the manuscript to eight copies and insisted it remain confidential.[414] It would stay secret and remain mostly unknown to the public for over a century. Published recognition of David's role has only recently appeared in academic writings since 1987,[415] and more widely since 1992 when a facsimile of the report was introduced and published.[416] Since then, David has received much credit for the forthcoming Swiss transition for reasons that will soon become apparent.

Chapter 10:

Emulation

"Our industry races towards the greatest danger and it is up to us to face the truth courageously and not give in to a false sense of safety by cherishing illusions which are no longer possible."

-Jacques David, 1877

"Fools find no pleasure in understanding but delight in airing their own opinions."

-Proverbs 18:2

Switzerland – January 1877

Much like Francis Cabot Lowell's mills, David's plan was emulation, where the Swiss would use their strengths and limitations to develop a hybrid factory system that would accomplish the same outcome that Waltham had achieved using similar, but distinctly different methods.

Nominal Swiss factories began to form, but they were more like workshops with a small group of workers rather than an imitation of Waltham with hundreds or thousands of employees.[417] David noted that the Swiss system would be distinctly different than the American way, yet "enjoy the same qualities as those from American workshops; that is, uniformity of manufacture, exactness of proportions, uniform running, simple assembly and simple repair."[418]

True gains had to be made by adapting the technological advances and innovative environment to local cultural factors while using regional geographic conditions and human strengths to design an equal but different system. Thus, emulation by the Swiss was far superior to imitation, especially when implementing a factory system in a geographically and culturally diametric region, a world away from Boston.

The system that resulted, with few modifications, was the plan David had recommended in his report. A 1904 post-facto account captured in a travel journal would bear unmistakable similarities to the system for which David's report had called:

> *Formerly each man worked at home, but this system is giving way to another, also distinct from that of great factories (in which all portions of a watch are made under one roof), of which the town has but few. Each establishment obtains from a number of separate workshops (in which the division of labour is carried out to a remarkable extent) the different portions of a watch, puts them together, and then claims to have 'manufactured' it.*[419]

By 1882, there were eighty-three watchmaking 'factories' in the country. Most were little more than workshops; only 5% of the factories had greater than twenty workers.[420] Much of the sluggish response was probably attributable to Favre-Perret,[421] who wrote: "To conclude this brief examination of the horology industry display at the Philadelphia Exhibition, we are happy and proud to be able to declare that Switzerland indisputably occupies the first position for this branch of [luxury] industry. All the principal centers of manufacture in our country were represented with dignity, and leave with honour from the comparisons made with our rival countries."

If this did not do enough to make the watchmakers feel that drastic change was unnecessary, he also pointed out that the Swiss already used "a great number of machines, but we have never, other than rare exceptions, pushed their use as far as the Americans."[422] In other words, he suggested that the Swiss watchmakers were already doing much of the mechanization that the Americans were doing, they just needed to continue to expand their use. This could not have been further from the truth; the American watch factories were far in advance of anything the Swiss possessed.

Watchmaking moves to the cities

The entrepreneurs who decided to establish watch factories often had to move to new geographic areas where they encountered less resistance to the new system. They also needed a concentration of people, which was hard to find in many rural watchmaking districts. The advantage of a factory system meant the owners needed fewer skilled watchmakers. They could hire less skilled but trained local people to operate some of the machines wherever they established their factory.

In the pre-1876 era of cottage manufacturing, the canton of Neuchâtel was the primary watch-producing region, yet the stalwart resistance of the watchmakers in the area led factory entrepreneurs to move to other regions where the people cared less about tradition. Cities like Biel, Grenchen, and Solothurn at the base of the Jura mountains became centers of manufacturing, as well as the canton of Bern.[423]

The geographical shift was evident by 1913 when an author wrote: "The exodus to Canton Berne (Jura-Bernois) to the detriment of Geneva and Neuchatel, especially, is explained by the tardy building of manufactories [in those locations]."[424] As a result of this geographic relocation, Bern, and not Neuchâtel, became the eventual home to companies like Omega, Heuer (pre-cursor to TAG Heuer), and Rolex.[425]

Despite the start of a transition to a new industrial system, many of the new factory towns maintained a rural character. Some of the most complicated watches continued to be produced in areas with no towns at all.[426] The effect of factories on the landscape was much different than in America.

The factories appeared to be little more than houses and almost none used steam power and coal until the twentieth century, freeing the landscape of dark soot and smog. By 1884, only 6% of Swiss factories had any kind of coal or gas-powered motor.[427] Almost all power generation was hydraulic and came from small water-powered bucket-wheels as the factories established themselves on nearby rivers. Avoiding expensive engines reduced the transition costs and contributed to building smaller factories where less power was needed. There were no dams along the rivers that would have restricted the location of a factory, so it was common to find many of them quaintly lined up in succession along a Swiss river valley.[428] The entire system, including the picturesque factories, was distinctly Swiss.

Swiss factory life

The factory life of the Swiss worker was a vast divergence from the progressive but demanding Waltham. In addition to being significantly smaller, Swiss factories allowed workers to maintain an element of their independence and former working environment. The workers at the Longines factory operated similarly to Waltham workers yet with marked differences such as singing while working, which was absent from Waltham. "Each morning, a multitude of workers went from the village, crossed the small bridge over the Suze [River] and found their ancestral labour. Until evening the rustle of the lathes, cutting and drilling machines resounded in the workshops, punctuated now and then by the dull blows of the presses, and often drowned out by the melancholic or merry songs of the workers."[429]

At the famed luxury producer Patek, Philippe, & Co., the factory was a collection of subdivided rooms "because the Swiss have a great aversion to anything that seems like factory labor," wrote an American reporter in 1895. "The workmen are very skilled but have to be humored." In a marked divergence from the punctual Waltham, the Patek workers "keep no hours, but come and go as they please."[430]

One of the most interesting changes made in most factories was banning the consumption of alcohol and hangovers at work.[431] From a safety perspective, while interacting with machinery, the banning of alcohol would seem a requirement. However, the Swiss banned alcohol from a practical standpoint to gain efficiency in production. They had to close the experience and efficiency gap that Waltham and its professional, disciplined workforce was always improving. Some accounts from early Swiss factories explained the concern for alcohol and drinking while on duty. One Swiss worker recounted: "You leave work to have a look around for some wild mushrooms, which develops into a game of boules,[432] and often ends with a night on the town."[433]

This was enough of a problem among Swiss workers that both David and Bally were impressed with the lack of drunkenness at American factories. David wrote: "Drunkenness is absolutely forbidden and it is not tolerated in any factory. The workmen can use their evenings and Sundays in any suitable way, and it is rare that repressive measures have to be taken against them for this vice."[434] Bally added:

> How can prosperity be expected in watch-making, for example, a business which ought to be so organized…when it happens that one of the members of this series makes "blue Monday," and has a headache on Tuesday, then on Wednesday it is the turn of another…It is impossible for an industry to make progress, or even to maintain itself on such a basis. The American works like a clock. His soda-water and his tea give him no headache; and brandy does not brutalize his intellect.[435]

In totality, the Swiss factory's culture brought many benefits of Waltham's precision manufacturing, but it was not a copy. It resulted from remarkable foresight that imitating American factories in their structure and operation was unfeasible. The Swiss factory system satisfied many aspects of Swiss culture while operating within the structural confines of geography and limited capital.

Even so, the cultural resistance ensured the factory transition was not widespread for decades. By 1888, 74% of the 44,000 Swiss watchmakers still worked from home.[436] By 1905, only seven companies had greater than 500 employees, many of whom still worked from home workshops. Longines was the second largest with 853 workers, followed by Omega with 724 workers, both small in size compared to Waltham.[437]

It would take two generations before most Swiss watchmaking occurred under a factory system.[438] The scale of production never mirrored Waltham's. Even thirty years after the Centennial Exhibition, Longines produced 130,000 watches annually, a capability Waltham achieved by 1880. The lack of many large companies did not imply Longines dominated the Swiss industry either. Longines' 130,000 watches produced in 1905 accounted for only 1.4% of all Swiss watch exports.[439]

Educating a new generation of Swiss workers

David relied on the strong Swiss education system to map his ideas onto the culture. David envisioned using the network of trade schools to inject new manufacturing methods into the watchmakers' ways of doing business. Besides his report, David's influence on the watchmaking schools in Switzerland would have the most dramatic effect on the transformation of the watch industry.

Much of the groundwork for the educational movement was laid before the Centennial Exhibition. The first watchmaking school opened in Geneva in 1824, followed by subsequent schools in Saint Imier, Le Locle, Neuchâtel, Bienne, and Fleurier, all in operation by the time of the Centennial Exhibition.[440] The government also supported the idea of watchmaking schools in western Switzerland, seeing them as insurance of long-term economic viability for the watchmaking regions, noting: "the best way of achieving this aim is to have well organized and well run watchmaking schools."[441] Before the Centennial, the schools taught "not only the requisite mechanical operations...[but also] geometry, trigonometry, descriptive geometry, and drawing, and the general principles of mechanism fundamentally necessary to the higher branches of horology."[442]

Following the Centennial Exhibition, David saw the existing network of schools as a way to influence the entire watchmaking region by training a generation of Swiss on new production techniques. David first identified the criticality of the school network in his report, writing: "access must be made increasingly easy for all. Their influence is important for the progress which our industry needs to achieve."[443] At the time, the schools were only available to a few apprentices paying high tuition, making them somewhat elite.[444] David realized that this stifled the expansion of technical education and limited the pool of potential students and innovators.

In his report, he also recommended changes to all watchmaking schools' curriculum: "It is essential that the pupils of these schools are educated in the use of the tools and machines employed by the [American] companies of whose improvements we have spoken, and that they are given the concepts of these new systems of manufacture."[445] In 1877, following the publication of his report, David proposed a new national curriculum that emphasized the new production methods, but his proposal was overruled by those who ran the schools. They overwhelmingly concluded that the only way to defeat the American threat was to further focus on traditional watchmaking methods to promote the work's art.[446]

Undeterred, David oversaw the implementation of his proposed curriculum at the school in his region of Saint Imier, where he served on the board. As historian Pierre-Yves Donze noted, this made David perhaps the first and *only person* to initially implement a factory system curriculum at a Swiss watchmaking school.[447] The curriculum at Saint Imier became a model for the other schools, which all soon adopted the changes made by David once it became apparent that the industry was quickly embracing the industrial concept.

For example, in 1878, the school at La-Chaux-de-Fonds admitted the need to train mechanics and committed to following the Saint Imier model. By 1882, students at La-Chaux-de-Fonds were already visiting factories as part of their curriculum.[448] Throughout the 1880s, the other watchmaking schools continued to adopt the model implemented by David at Saint Imier.[449] Initially, the schools were private philanthropic ventures, but following the transformation and expansion of access, they became primarily government funded as an economic necessity.[450]

David's curriculum was different because it emphasized the use of the machine, which became an art form within Switzerland. If the American system moved towards using unskilled workers to operate the machines, the Swiss sought to professionalize the machine operators. Another Centennial delegation member suggested that "when a workman who possesses the spirit of order, some training and the elementary principles of geometry and mechanics, has charge of an automatic machine, his mind cannot be at rest. When his machine is in operation, he profits by his leisure to examine the work which it has performed. He detects and remedies the causes which make it irregular."[451] In the Swiss view, they needed more than just operators, rather well-trained machinists who could translate the product of mass production machines into Swiss horological art.[452]

Forces at work

While influential, Jacques David and his report were not the only factors catalyzing or contributing to the Swiss watch industry's transformation. Many of the details and full capabilities of American companies as reported by David were shocking, but the Swiss watchmakers and the government already knew there was a problem well before the Centennial Exhibition. In early 1876, before David's trip to America, the local government offered a contest to find solutions to the impending watch industry crisis, which was evident from reduced exports.[453]

The formation of the Intercantonal Society of Jura Industries (SIIJ) in May 1876 was an early response to the growing predicament. Theo Gribi had been commissioned as early as April 1876 to search for answers. Even some of the information in David's report was already known by the Swiss but viewed as inconsequential. For example, earlier in 1876, another watchmaker would make similar proposals to those contained in David's report. Therefore, David's ideas were not entirely novel.[454]

Nor can the shock of Philadelphia be seen as the sole catalyst for change in the watch industry. As Marti noted, "the importance of the Philadelphia Exhibition in 1876, which is often quoted as a trigger for the introduction of new production models [in Switzerland], should be considered with caution."[455] Despite this, the Centennial's impression on watchmakers such as David and Favre-Perret cannot be ignored either.

Before 1876, there were almost no factories except the Longines experiment. By 1882, eighty-three factories would be in operation, increasing to 170 factories by 1888.[456] The effect of the Centennial and David's report on the watchmakers is even credited by the modern watch industry literature as being the stimulus for change: "The report [David] writes upon his return is generally regarded as being the catalyst for the industrialization of Swiss watchmaking."[457]

David's effect on the Swiss transformation from industrial espionage and his subsequent report and leadership was significant and the watch industry as known today would probably not exist if the events of 1876 never took place. But these changes only accounted for manufacturing. The Swiss needed more than just a factory system, which only addressed manufacturing inefficiencies. Waltham had a twenty-year advantage, seemingly unlimited capital, and a newly solidified global reputation for quality. The odds could not have been against David any further. Yet, his recommendations and those of Favre-Perret and a few others would guide the Swiss watchmakers' strategy to a much stronger position heading into the turbulent and quickly changing global market of the 1880s and 1890s.

Chapter 11

Scheme of Maneuver

"We have shown you the means by which we believe we can prevent being overrun by this powerful and bold competition from overseas, and we believe it our duty to particularly insist on the imminence of this danger. We can affirm that there will need to be a considerable united effort and much work to regain lost time."

-Jacques David, 1877

Switzerland – 1877 to 1887

While the Swiss producers were beginning to recalibrate, Waltham was making simultaneous moves in blissful ignorance of the changes taking place in Switzerland. The next ten years, from 1877 to 1887, would prove pivotal as many competitors in the global watch market made strategic moves that appeared small at the time but would usher in far-reaching consequences in the decades to follow. During this period, Waltham and the Swiss would each evaluate the outcome of the Centennial and the strategic situation as they saw it. By the close of the decade following the Centennial, Waltham and the Swiss would each chart a new strategic course, putting them on very different trajectories.

The Swiss strategy

The Swiss' choice of where to compete was guided by the reality of where Waltham had the most market share. Waltham focused on the affordable segment of the market with watches that were cheap but also known for quality. Waltham's geographic reach covered the most significant markets, including India, Japan, Australia, South America, England, and Russia. David aptly recognized that the Swiss could not compete on price in America given the high tariffs placed on Swiss watches. With Waltham having found a successful scope selling cheaper watches, David was sure that Waltham would continue to manufacture the most affordable watches going forward.[458]

David also recognized something about the American market of which Waltham and Elgin seemed to be ignorant. He realized the American companies were in a withering price war that would cripple the Swiss if they tried to compete while simultaneously trying to transition to an industrial system. In David's view, the American strategy was to push the Swiss from the market by continuously lowering prices while campaigning for the United States to maintain protective tariffs. As an ominous foreshadow, he wrote: "It appears difficult for such an impertinent undertaking to continue seriously for a long time, because a result of this fight is that the principal factories must sell too cheaply" to remain profitable.[459]

Accordingly, David actively discouraged the Swiss watchmakers from focusing any efforts on America's affordable market segment. David saw the low-cost American market as a trap for imprudent Swiss producers. If the Swiss tried to win the affordable segment, they would not only "lose the American market, from which they will be excluded sooner or later by the force of events, but also to be excluded from other regions of the world" as Swiss manufacturers chased each other into insolvency.[460] Favre-Perret also said as much, declaring: "We must therefore make up our minds to lose the American market!"[461]

One major contribution of Favre-Perret was his identification of the potential for the Swiss to regain and maintain their supremacy as luxury watchmakers. He identified that luxury Swiss watches still garnered admiration and encouraged the Swiss to continue competing in the luxury market. He noted: "Switzerland has preserved the monopoly of small watches and appears to have only England as a serious competitor for complicated watches."[462] He also observed: "our competitors cannot create the army of artists and true horologists which we have and who are essential to finish high-quality watches. We are consequently in a better position, and we hope and do not doubt that the Swiss will be able to profit."[463]

Between their two reports, which were the most prominent documents to emerge from the watchmakers' experience at the Centennial Exhibition, David and Favre-Perret collectively identified the strategic roadmap that would lead to a Swiss recovery and could largely be seen in the decades to come. The strategic road would follow four main objectives:

1) Restore the Swiss' reputation through legal enforcement of claims on gold and silver content
2) Improve the overall mechanical reliability of Swiss watches
3) Do not rely on the American market; shift to a global market emphasis
4) Focus on Swiss strengths of fine craftsmanship, finishing, and adjusting associated with luxury watches

Enforcing quality in Swiss production

One of the most basic things David called for was penalties for Swiss producers who fraudulently hallmarked their products by claiming higher gold or silver content. Remedying this problem was the first step to restoring consumer confidence and would be a prerequisite to any plan for global competition. In his report, one of David's recommended responses was collective action by the watchmakers to look into ways to regulate "silver and gold; if this solution is applied sufficiently [and] energetically [it will]...put an end to the abuses which are made and which continue with impunity under the current system." He called for "much larger penalties [which] are necessary, and we hope for a rigorous law this year that will put an end to those practices by dishonest persons which give such a poor reputation to our country."[464]

David's idea was not novel, rather he added to an ongoing chorus of watchmakers who were calling for a solution to this known and embarrassing problem.[465] Leading up to the Centennial, many dishonest watchmakers had saturated the market with watches that alleged high gold or silver content while being fraudulent and mechanically unreliable, contributing to the 'buyer beware' reputation of the Swiss. Even the official report from the Centennial noted: "the very name of a Swiss watch began to be indicative of its worthless character."[466]

In 1880, Francillon contributed to implementing the enforcement suggested by David. While acting as Longines' principal owner, he also served in the regional government (1877 to 1881) and the national government (1881 to 1890) where he kept a watchful eye on policies that affected the watch industry. Using his

158

role as a member of the regional and then national government, Francillon helped draft a bill that created local control offices for managing gold and silver markings.[467]

Francillon's proposal was adopted almost in its entirety across Switzerland.[468] The law created a system of enforcement for the markings of gold and silver watches that guaranteed their content. By the early twentieth century, the law had the intended effect and consumers began to believe that a Swiss gold watch was made with the stated content. In 1913, a visitor to Switzerland observed: "The federal government has established a control over gold and silver goods, thus every good watch is hall-marked, which is a preventative against cheating."[469]

While the certification for gold and silver focused mostly on the outer watch case, the Swiss also needed a way to vouch for the reliability of the inner workings of the watch, which American models far surpassed. David advocated for establishing and enforcing standards for accuracy in performance. He suggested the Swiss watchmakers create a professional association that would police the industry and its watchmakers' marketing claims. He recommended that watchmakers adhere to agreed-upon quality control principles that customers could expect when buying any reputable Swiss watch.

To ensure a measure of enforcement, David called for the official certification of watches, providing a document of guarantee. He insisted that "No certificate would be issued to a watch unless it bears the name of the manufacturer in an obvious place decided by regulation… There will be no certificates for watches below a certain degree of quality."[470] By requiring names on watches, brands would now be publicly responsible for their work, which would ideally encourage excellence through pride. Watches that were certified for their performance earned a certificate that was a mark of quality for customers.

This did not completely solve the quality control problem; there was still rampant counterfeiting and poorly made Swiss watches, but at least the superior watches could be identified. To ensure that global markets were aware of the stringently enforced standards of quality, David called for a collective marketing campaign on behalf of those producers who met quality standards. David observed that previously, advertisements had promoted "bad merchandise as much if not more than good products, and the public has every right to be wary of [Swiss advertisements]." He envisioned that "We would cease being tacitly responsible to foreigners for the frauds which are done in Switzerland on case hallmarks, quality and the names and denominations of movements."[471]

Through strict standards of enforcement and well-advertised claims of quality, the name 'Swiss Made' eventually became one of the world's most prestigious marquees of excellence that survives into the modern era. A 2016 study found that consumers are willing to pay up to twice as much for a watch bearing these words.[472] Many premium watches still carry the moniker 'Officially Certified,' including Rolex watches.

Official certification was an important step for aiding in marketing claims, but it had diminishing returns from a practical product performance perspective. By 1876, the best Waltham watches and many of the luxury Swiss watches displayed at the Centennial performed to the same standard that most of the best mechanical watches perform today. This did not stop the Swiss from advertising the importance of accuracy found in "officially certified" watches. The advertised levels of accuracy far exceeded the needs of the average Gilded Age customer and were more precise than most people would ever require of a watch, even today. Yet, the emphasis on certification demonstrated that the Swiss acknowledged the need to show customers that the Swiss watchmakers had changed their ways.

Choosing where to compete

Even with a better product, David and Favre-Perret doubted that the Swiss could ever compete against Waltham in the American market. The Swiss conclusion to abandon the American market largely resulted from high tariffs driven by protectionist sentiments. While the tariffs served to protect Waltham, they forced the Swiss to look abroad to other markets, ultimately reducing the competition from foreign competitors in America.

Early in Waltham's history, tariffs provided the company with space and time needed to develop as a dominate producer. By the time of the Centennial, the tariff was 25%, putting the Swiss at a strong disadvantage. In America, protectionism and tariffs were viewed as patriotic requirements necessary to nurture infant industries. Following the Centennial, a Chicago newspaper communicated the sentiment, writing that the results of Waltham's success as a company "shows that American industry only wants a fair start and an even chance to win against the world and proves the value of the protective policy."[473]

Prominent American politician James G. Blaine, a senator from Maine argued in 1880 that the tariff was not strictly intended to raise government revenue, but rather to stifle foreign producers selling goods within American borders. More broadly, Blaine argued for the successes brought by protectionism: "the prosperity of the American people has been enormously developed by reason of the tariff." Blaine viewed the American watch industry as the pinnacle of protectionist success.[474]

Waltham's contemporaries viewed the tariffs as necessary and constructive for domestic companies. On the contrary, economist Douglas Irwin concluded that "trade protection was probably not a key factor behind U.S. economic growth in the late nineteenth century." Irwin pointed out that many people still view the nineteenth-century tariffs as good for American industrial growth, writing: "the association between high tariffs and rapid output growth is frequently noted in such a way as to leave the distinct impression that such causation is highly likely, or at least that the nineteenth-century experience demonstrates that protectionism was not a bad economic policy."[475]

The lack of meaningful inventive competition from the Swiss in the low-cost market created a long-term hazard for Waltham's prospects at home and abroad. While the Swiss began innovating better products that would attract sales, Waltham focused on cutting costs to win the price war against Elgin. As a result, a Milwaukee newspaper noted that by 1882, the Swiss were again making better ordinary watches than Waltham. The writer observed: "the Swiss manufacturers have done what…they must to succeed, and the American companies have not improved the quality of their work."[476]

At this point, it was apparent that the Swiss had not been scared away by the Centennial; instead, they were frighteningly inspired. Royal Robbins was about to discover that his enemy was not running; they had regrouped and were now attacking. Had Waltham not been decisively engaged in a war of attrition with Elgin, Robbins might have discerned that the Swiss were almost in a position to overrun the powerful, innovative Waltham.

Chapter 12:

War on All Fronts

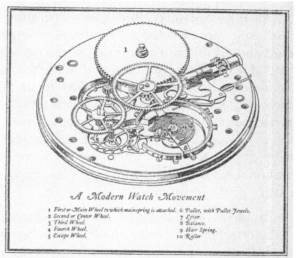

A mechanical watch movement and major parts ('Time Telling Through the Ages,' Public Domain)

Waltham – 1877 to 1887

The decade following the Centennial Exhibition had started with Waltham as a seemingly dominant industrial producer who achieved prominence, recognition, and fame. Yet the proceeding years brought about increasing competition and diminishing profits despite improving economic conditions following the Panic of 1873. It began to show that Waltham's novel production system and outsized success in the first twenty-five years of its operations was not sustainable given the current competitive dynamic or the company's chosen strategy.

False comfort

As 1877 began, Waltham was operating in the glow of well-earned hubris. Newspapers worldwide reported about Waltham's stunning performance at the Centennial Exhibition. Robbins told shareholders that the Centennial "called public attention to us and our superior methods and our superior goods with an effect otherwise unattainable."[477] The excitement drove people to demand Waltham's watches in increasing numbers, especially international customers. International sales evolved into a critical ingredient in Waltham's profit formula.

In early 1877, Robbins informed shareholders that, "The effect of our Centennial Exhibit is being felt in a daily enlargement of our list of foreign customers, as well as in a confirmation of our popularity at home. Our foreign trade is now fully one quarter of our total business, and seems to be growing in all directions."[478] A year later in 1878, he again emphasized the effect of the Centennial on sales, writing: "Undoubtedly the Centennial Exhibition [and the display] of our goods may be credited with good effects upon both our domestic and foreign business."[479] Sales data from the year following the Centennial showed undoubtable growth.[480]

In 1878, Robbins wrote confidently of the demise of the Swiss, demonstrating his blissful ignorance of the ongoing transformation. The Centennial had elicited the perception he had hoped for: that of a dominant company that had already defeated an artisanal adversary through technological superiority. "The truth is [Waltham's] efforts have resulted in supplanting to a most hopeful degree in the market our old and powerful enemies the Swiss."[481]   He wrote confidently that Waltham was so powerful that Swiss merchants now imported Waltham's watches. He then compared Waltham to an occupying army in a statement that served to highlight the folly that was to follow: "And where we go [to Switzerland] we stay and multiply."[482] With the Swiss no longer an apparent strategic concern, Robbins turned his full attention towards solidifying Waltham's dominant position as the largest, most prestigious producer of watches among the other technologically advanced American competitors.

Waltham ignores the luxury market

Following the Centennial Exhibition, Waltham had a unique opportunity to move toward the luxury market. Its watches had outdone the most-respected Swiss timepieces and Waltham advertised the victory in seemingly every American newspaper. However, the company never successfully moved towards the luxury market even though it made some excellent products and the luxury segment offered higher profits.

After winning an award (with its *AWC* model) at the Centennial for producing the best luxury watches in the world, Robbins did not use Waltham's fame to move up-market to compete against the luxury Swiss watches. Instead, Robbins viewed the Centennial as a referendum on the supremacy of the American machine-made watch. A widely circulated 1877 Waltham advertisement documented Favre-Perret "confessing the triumph of American Machine [made]

Watches over the Swiss hand-made watches." Note that Waltham was not the focus of the chosen statement.[483] Specifically, it did not mention Waltham's unique triumph over all competitors, including other American companies. Instead, Robbins appeared to have seen the results of the Centennial as a way to show customers that Waltham was part of a superior genre of machine-made products that performed better than the Swiss masters.[c]

An example of Waltham using the Centennial to promote its watches in general rather than its luxury, award-winning watches could be seen in an advertisement from New Orleans in 1877. As an introduction, the advertisement noted that Waltham's "watches" won an award, with no specific mention of the model. The ad then explained: "These watches claimed four different awards at Philadelphia, over and above all watches, either foreign or American manufacture."

The advertisement then proceeded to show the "revised and reduced" price list, with the most expensive watch shown being $90, most of which was accounted for in the 18-karat gold case, not the watch itself. The "silver watch" that dominated the advertisement sold for a low price of $14 at retail.[484] The highlighted products and prices were directionally opposite of the award-winning *AWC* model. Thus, Waltham's victory with its luxury watches at the Centennial was not used to capture specific advantages among luxury buyers, rather they were used to promote

---

[c] This appears to be an unusual decision, but Robbins' motivation leading up to the Centennial was to demonstrate that the machine-made watch was superior; thus the advertising approach fit within his broader strategy.

the general reliability of Waltham's product portfolio, reinforcing the themes of 'cheap and reliable.'

At the time, Robbins' decision to ignore the luxury market seemed to be a wise proposition by providing the market with exactly what consumers demanded. Sales history and current economic conditions showed that American consumers overwhelmingly preferred cheap, reliable, mass-produced watches over luxury ones. The low-margin, high-volume sales of cheap watches appeared to be the most-promising source of future profits.

A prominent news journal commented on Waltham's commitment to the segment, noting: "As yet the Waltham Watch Company [has] not gone largely into the manufacture of the very highest class of watches, the great demand being for good time keepers at a reasonable price."[485] The journal implied that Waltham's focus was the future of profitable manufacturing: "The Americans to all appearance will soon have the command of the traffic in watches all over the world."[486]

Defending against Elgin

As competition intensified, Waltham's main concern was Elgin along with the seemingly infinite number of competitors entering the market. Robbins told investors in 1878: "The competition in the prices of low grade goods which has recently been renewed between the Elgin Company and ourselves is a matter just now of so much pecuniary interest to us and of inquiry on the part of our stockholders that I feel it my duty to give you a brief statement of its history and present aspect."[487] The competition was cutthroat and

169

called for more than a free market could provide. Robbins thought he found a solution: collusion.

Collectively, Waltham and Elgin controlled about 80% of the American watch market.[488] Collusion was not yet illegal in the United States, which naturally invited price fixing. This was not out of the ordinary for the era, especially when withering competition threatened the survival of entire industries. Many industry titans, including John D. Rockefeller, viewed competition as a recipe for insolvency. Even when writing in 1945, Waltham biographer Charles Moore implied that the eventual Sherman Anti-Trust Act (1890) and the vilification of collusion were naïve.[489]

Before 1878, Waltham and Elgin maintained verbal agreements on pricing, always promising to notify the other if one intended to lower the prices of its goods. However, the Panic of 1873 strained the companies' ability to maintain profitable sales, especially as the depression lasted in earnest for over six years. In 1878, Elgin defected from the agreement by lowering its prices without giving Waltham ample warning. Robbins complained: "the Elgin Company suddenly reduced without notice to us its lower grades of goods about 25 per cent. Verbal understandings prior to that time made such notice a duty."[490] Robbins further complained: "we observed [the agreement] in good faith. The Elgin Co. on the contrary secretly began their preparations to make a very low grade movement." The collusive agreements resulted from an increasing focus on price instead of quality.

Waltham loss and Swiss gain in international markets

Finding intense competition within American borders, Waltham looked overseas for more sales. The company had traditionally found success in the ever-expanding international markets. In 1876, before the Centennial, international sales for Waltham were "grow[ing] steadily."[491] By 1877, they accounted for 25% of company revenues.[492] However, a retooling Swiss industry would soon be able to export similar machine-made watches to these same markets for which Waltham relied for continued growth. The low wages in Switzerland combined with more efficient production meant that they could produce and sell reliable watches to global markets significantly cheaper than Waltham. The quickly intensifying effect of the Swiss in global markets could be seen within about eight years following the Centennial Exhibition.

Waltham's last positive report about international sales growth occurred in 1882, with international sales accounting for 33% of revenues.[493] Even Robbins' 1878 excitement about exporting watches to Switzerland with plans to "stay and multiply" like an occupying army was quickly dampened. By 1882, the American Consul in Switzerland reported that imports of American watches to Switzerland had ceased.[494]

The quickly recovering Swiss industry was captured in an 1885 newspaper that recounted: "having seen their American market almost escape them after the Centennial Exhibition in 1876, [the Swiss] were able by the employment of the greatest energy, perseverance and skill to regain what they had lost, and even to increase their export of watches to a point never before reached."[495]

171

In 1886, Robbins would complain: "Competition however is very severe and is proceeding from sources more numerous than ever. To say nothing of foreign manufacturers we have the following list of domestic makers to meet..." whom he implied were an obvious and recurring concern of shareholders.[496] In 1888, Waltham was forced to close some of its international offices. By 1891, international sales had shrunk to 11% of revenue, never returning to 1882 levels of success, indicating that Waltham's overseas growth had been stunted. [497]

Less than twenty-five years after the Centennial, it was obvious that the Swiss had successfully diversified their sales and target markets away from America. Prior to 1876, the United States accounted for 20% to 25% of Swiss watch exports; in the years to come, Switzerland's former 'milk cow' would only account for 2.4% of Swiss watch exports by value. Furthermore, the Swiss would send fewer watches to America than they had in 1872.[498] Instead, the Swiss turned to non-U.S. markets for most of their sales. Many of the newly found sources of Swiss prosperity were Waltham's previous growth markets, where the Swiss now had a production-cost advantage devoid of the American tariffs. [499]

The Swiss' decision to avoid the American market and focus internationally was a clear and significant strategic choice. It brought almost immediate consequences for Waltham, who could no longer look overseas for future sales and provided the Swiss with profitable outlets devoid of serious competition.

With intense competition at home and resurgent Swiss competition abroad, Waltham found its profits severely hampered, even with the aid of collusive agreements. While gross profitability showed that Waltham had its most profitable year to date in 1882, the profit margin was only 12%.[500] This was compared to 1860 to 1881 when the average profit margin exceeded 20%.[501] While sales of Waltham's watches increased from 66,000 watches annually in 1873 to 230,000 in 1882, the general trend in profitability had been precipitously declining.[502] Waltham was acutely feeling the effects of competition and margin compression in the 'cheap and reliable' market segment. By the mid-1880s, it was evident that Waltham needed to change.

Chapter 13:

Change of Command

Ezra Fitch ('Timing a Century', Public Domain)

Waltham Factory – 1883 to 1893

In 1883, Waltham hired a new superintendent to take over the factory's daily management from Charles Vander Woerd. He had proved to be a good inventor but not an able executive.

The new superintendent, Ezra Fitch, was "a little man, quiet and friendly; he took pains to speak to every employee regardless of position, and he was always

175

accessible to anyone who wished to see him."[503] Fitch had sixteen years of experience in sales and was also a skilled watchmaker who would accumulate twenty-nine patents during his lifetime.[504] His resume was described as an "unusual combination of talents" and "exactly what the position of general manager required."[505] While he was an inventor, he was primarily a salesman in the execution of his duties.[506] In other industries, the sales staff often drove production and investment decisions, so Fitch's appointment appeared a natural step in Waltham's progression.[507]

By 1883, it was apparent that Waltham was not operating free as a definitive market leader as some might have hoped following its stunning performance at the Centennial Exhibition. Accordingly, Fitch was hired to do much more than oversee the factory or its production. As a salesman, it was implied that Fitch was not in his new role to discover novel methods of production, rather his job was to closely align what the market demanded and manufacture those products. Unlike the inventor Vander Woerd, Fitch was a professional businessman who would ardently search for methods to improve profitability by both increasing sales and cutting costs.

Evolution in management trends

Fitch soon took a seat on the board of directors in 1884, an arrangement non-existent with previous superintendents.[508] Fitch's appointment began a marked change in how the company formulated its strategy as well. After Fitch's ascension as superintendent, "Factory executives accepted without any resistance the subordinate position assigned to them."[509] By 1886,

Fitch would also be appointed to the dual role of president of the company, thus having control over both the strategic and operational (production) direction.[510] In the Fitch era, Robbins's control began to dwindle and was observed to be effectively shared with Fitch starting in 1883.[511]

Robbins was still the treasurer, but his input became nominal.[512] This was evident in his annual reports to shareholders. The reports no longer showed detailed analysis and well-considered strategic plans for the future. By 1886, his previously exhaustive annual reports, which outlined significant strategic objectives, became perfunctory at best and demonstrated a divergence from the previous twenty-six years. His reports indicated that he no longer viewed himself as responsible for reporting the strategic direction of the company. The change in tone was commensurate with the restructuring of company leadership that had taken place.

Historian Alfred Chandler would note that the railroad industry led the way in the evolution of corporate management structure in the late nineteenth century. The changes at Waltham appeared to follow the developments in managerial trends. In the railroad industry, Chandler observed that the president and the board of directors began to represent large and more anonymous shareholders rather than close advisors.[513] Board members were "successful businessmen in their own right who served the [the company] on a part-time basis, [and] were almost always either large investors or spokesmen for investors."[514]

As delegates of the stockholders, the *president's* and the *board's* primary focus was on the financial returns of the investment to guarantee a proper dividend.[515] In contrast, the *managers'* job (similar to the superintendent at Waltham) was to maintain a long-term focus on developing technologies that would sustain the company's capabilities into the future, creating a natural and enduring tension between management and short-term shareholders.[516]

As in the railroads, Waltham's shareholder base grew and became increasingly diversified in the 1880s. Under Fitch, Waltham became progressively focused on profitability by lowering unit costs of production. However, unlike the railroads, Waltham did not have a superintendent focused on long-term innovation at the expense of short-term profitability. With Fitch serving as both president and superintendent for the forthcoming eighteen years, there was no natural tension between immediate profits and costly innovative experimentation. The company became short-term focused in both its factory operations and strategic direction.

Fitch's tenure showed the company spiraling in a direction from which it could never recover. Waltham biographer Charles Moore called 1883 and the appointment of Fitch the "end of the Golden Age" for Waltham.[517] As he began to take over more responsibility for Waltham's strategic direction, the company started to show desperation as large investments continued to yield smaller and smaller profit margins.[518]

Losing its innovative edge

Because of the decreasing profit margins, Waltham continued to make large factory investments to lower its unit costs of production. Fitch committed

Waltham even further to the 'cheap and reliable' consumer segment by burdening the company with an enormous factory with thousands of machines committed to producing specific models of watches. These expenditures created an asset-heavy organization that was less nimble and responsive to the quickly changing industry and consumer demand for watches during the 1880s and 1890s.

In 1883, Robbins complained that the capital investment projects served as an "obstruction and distraction" noting that the "building works have interfered still more with the profit & loss account."[519] Robbins' complaints were not enough to stop the spending, which disproportionately increased in subsequent years. Fitch "believed in taking full advantage of every opportunity for expansion," while Robbins was known for being aggressive in the execution of strategy but conservative in his use of money.[520]

From 1884 to 1888, the company invested forcefully in new production capability, with machinery assets increasing 218% in the brief four-year period. Waltham also continued to internally produce the latest mechanical production efficiencies at great expense to the company. The capital investments yielded no additional competitive advantages as competitors simply copied the efficiency improvements.[521]

Waltham's employees had historically produced innovations that made the company an industry leader in managerial methods, machines, and final products. Waltham had always focused on experimentation that reduced the cost of production through better management, machinery, and simplified watch designs, but these also resulted in radically novel inventions.[522]

179

Moore noted that when Waltham was founded under Dennison, "inventors took over the responsibility for production and continued their search for better equipment and methods. They were very successful, both as managers of production and as inventors."[523] Robbins sustained that culture. Under the leadership of men like Ambrose Webster and Charles Vander Woerd, innovation drove Waltham's success.[524] Prior to Fitch's tenure, the company was considered a "fountainhead of technical knowledge."[525]

This changed in 1883. Fitch "brought a marked change in general policy; then the inventors...had to subordinate their wishes to the dictates of the sales department."[526] He instituted new policies that ensured "factory personnel could no longer follow the path of inspiration at a leisurely pace; instead, they were driven to performance of a task in research and development which was *set by their competitors* and driven by the selling staff."[527] (author's emphasis). This statement emphasized that Waltham was now rapidly responding to tactical-level actions by competitors rather than succeeding as a strategic leader. Accordingly, Fitch ensured employees focused strictly on the products that would sell rather than exploring innovations.[528] Despite the many famous Waltham inventors who would work under Fitch, the company forfeited its greatest strengths of managerial and process innovation.

The 1921 Harvard Business School study

The effects of Fitch's change in policy on managerial and process innovation could be seen in a before-and-after comparison, looking at David's 1876 report when compared to a 1921 Harvard Business

School study, both of which analyzed managerial operations in depth. The writer, George Blow, spent time at the Waltham factory interviewing managers who recounted company procedures. Blow's study showed a remarkable regression in managerial processes from 1876 to 1921, with Waltham being a victim of problems it had successfully conquered and was an industry leader in solving decades prior.

For example, Blow reported that in 1908 a new middle manager attempted to institute the scientific Taylor system of job cards, which were designed to strictly cost-account for employee times of machine operation on specific parts. According to Blow, this system was not in use at the company and encountered resistance upon implementation. Resistance to Taylorism was not entirely out of the ordinary on a broader cultural scale as workers disdained the system, which imposed strict output requirements, usually for the benefit of the owners with little reward for the worker.[529]

In Blow's words, Waltham implemented, "a system of control of work by means of job cards and [a] control board adopted. Up till recently the new system had not [been] met with the wholehearted approval and cooperation of all the members of the management and hence its development had not progressed with very great rapidity [up to 1921]."[530] Blow also reported, "Due to this reason, and to the fact that *there has been no scientific time study made on any of the jobs*, there is considerable discrepancy in the rates and the amounts received per unit of time." (Author's emphasis).[531] This summary of operations and descriptions of resistance to adopting modern procedures is remarkable in light of David's report on similar subjects.

In 1876, Waltham had an advanced system of tracking inputs to watch production. While not entirely to the standards of Taylor's scientific management, the 1876 system used by Waltham and described by David demonstrated a system far in advance of that reported by Blow in 1921. David wrote about Waltham:

> *In each workshop bulletins accompany the work. These bulletins show for each job the name of the workman, the date of reception of the work, and the number of parts received...This bulletin, which has all the elements to price the work, is collected by the workshop office and a new bulletin is provided for the following task...When a batch of parts is finished in the workshop, the bulletins attached to this batch make it possible to price it exactly...The work of the central office is very complicated and the offices at Waltham and Elgin are extremely large. It continuously keeps control of work and records all the communications of the foremen relating to the cost of work...*[532]

The job cards described by Blow and the bulletins described by David were different, but both had an emphasis on efficiency and the ability to time-cost production. According to Blow's study, Waltham was a slow adopter which was noteworthy given David's descriptions of Waltham's managerial practices which pointed to Waltham moving towards scientific management a full quarter century before Taylor coined the practice.

Overall, the company's strategies implemented under Fitch resulted in no profitable gains, nor did other minor attempts to improve the company's position.

Moore observed that many strategies were tried, "not in a casual or hasty fashion, but with thoroughness and precision which were notable for that period."[533]

One of the most substantial problems brought by a strategy of trying to capture value through cutting innovation is that "tactics oriented to capturing value could have long-run negative consequences by distracting the firm from needed investments in value creation. Further, such tactics may be inappropriate because they are inconsistent with organizational values."[534] This succinctly described the crux of Waltham's dilemma. The company was so focused on cutting costs that it began ignoring the precepts that made it successful in its early days.

With all attempts to cut costs appearing to be exhausted, Waltham had increasingly fewer options if it was to remain the industry leader of 'cheap and reliable' watches. The strategic decisions it had made up to this point were now bearing consequences. It had invested heavily in assets, hindered its innovative culture, ignored the much smaller but more profitable luxury segment, and found intense competition from imitators at home and the Swiss in its overseas markets.

The once-novel company with a significant competitive advantage appeared to have only one remaining option. The consumer wanted cheaper products, and the only way this was possible was through impossible economies of scale or by producing a much cheaper, less reliable, minimally viable product.

Chapter 14:

Overrun

Waltham watch dial from 1903 (Author's photo)

"As to the future nothing worth saying occurs to me ... Competition however is very severe and is proceeding from sources more numerous than ever."

-Royal Robbins, 1886

The Global Market – 1893 to 1900

While Waltham was implementing new strategies that attempted to regain its competitive advantage, the Swiss were responding with increasing success. Though not widespread in acceptance, the emergent Swiss transformation was proving to be almost immediately successful, especially with regard to the implied scope, or where the Swiss chose to compete in the market.

Using the hybrid factory system akin to the Waltham method of mass production, the Swiss watchmakers increased their output from 1.6 million watches in 1876, to 3 million by 1886 and would achieve an output of 8 million watches by 1905.[535] In particular, the Swiss had managed to diversify away from their primary market, growing sales outside the United States.

The Swiss capture the luxury market for good

Switzerland expanded its hold on the luxury watch market as well. The Swiss effectively, though not completely, abandoned the *affordable* watch segment in America to Waltham and Elgin, who maintained a dominant position. Meanwhile, the high reputation in the *luxury* market undoubtedly belonged to the Swiss. It was Favre-Perret who had told the watchmakers: "our competitors cannot create the army of artists and true horologists which we have and who are essential to finish watches of high quality. We are consequently in a better position, and we hope and do not doubt that the Swiss will be able to profit."[536]

The Swiss, particularly the masters of Geneva, were known for producing some of the finest luxury watches and works of art since the seventeenth century. The Swiss watch had become preferred by the wealthy over the much thicker English watches due to the Swiss penchant for thin construction, something that was important for the European clothing styles of the day which were tighter than previous generations. Landes noted: "[Much thicker English] watches were no problem as long as they were hung around the neck or suspended from belts; but when it became customary to wear them in pockets, thickness became an inconvenience."[537]

Luxury watchmakers such as Vacheron Constantin, Patek, Philippe & Co, Jürgensen, Matile, or Ekegren were known for their masterpieces. The Centennial Exhibition judges captured the sentiment surrounding some of Switzerland's premier luxury makers, who were known for their craftsmanship both before and during the Centennial. In describing Patek, Philippe, & Co, the judges wrote: "Besides the watches of ordinary grades, this house has long had an excellent reputation for skill in the manufacture of fully-adjusted movements, and for the artistic decoration of the cases of their watches."[538]

To maintain the luxury market following the Centennial, the Swiss convinced consumers that seemingly irrational spending on luxury watches provided something that Waltham could not. The Swiss were able to do so through a few small but consequential differences in strategy.

Waltham's watches were seen as affordable products, and while this had an appeal for the average consumer, it was neither elite nor signaled wealth. Many Swiss luxury watches were complicated in their mechanism, featuring date, day, and moon phase functions, something few Waltham models integrated. These complicated watches were a rare but obvious sign of conspicuous consumption, as knowledge of the moon phase or date mattered to few. Even after the Centennial, the judges observed: "[the Swiss] can certainly expect to hold the undisputed control of the manufacture of all kinds of complicated watches. In this field of production they are without rivals."[539]

The Swiss positioned themselves as makers of fine, accurate watches in their marketing. Meanwhile, Waltham emphasized that it was the cheapest and most reliable. Waltham's advertisements from the 1880s and early 1890s showed a deliberate effort to obtain the growing middle-class customer:

"The American Waltham Watches...Being accurate, reliable and comparatively inexpensive, they offer the average buyer the best value obtained...The lower grades, although excellent time keepers, are sold so reasonably as to make it possible for almost every one to possess a good watch."

Meanwhile, Waltham's "higher grades" were described as *"durable and entirely satisfactory."* (1884).[540] Another advertisement noted that Waltham's watches were *"a fine timekeeper at a moderate price...the finest grades of movement are now sold at astonishingly low prices."* (1880).[541]

A third advertised on behalf of both Waltham and Elgin: *"CHEAP AND GOOD WATCHES."* (1880).[542]

The latter advertisement captured Waltham's market positioning strategy. The company continued to pursue the strategy even after obtaining fame at the Centennial for making the most accurate luxury watches in the world. Soon, the Waltham watch would become a bargain product:

"Waltham Watch $3.65. Only one to a customer." (1890).[543]

"Gold watches $15. Ladies 14kt Solid Gold Waltham watches at prices lower than elsewhere." (1891).[544]

Meanwhile, Swiss luxury watchmakers advertised using a completely different value proposition, much more reminiscent of what modern consumers associate with luxury products. Patek, Philippe, & Co claimed:

"No watch in history of horology has ever attained to such prominence…The most prominent jewelers of the United States now carry the Patek, Philippe, & Co as their best watch." (1891).[545]

One jeweler advertised: *"every year [Patek, Philippe, & Co has] obtained the prize medal which is annually awarded to the firm whose Watches had the best rating during the whole year."* (1886).[546]

Another jeweler boasted of being the *"sole agent for…the celebrated Patek, Philippe & Co's Watches which have no superior in the world, and while being in the equal to the Jules Jurgenson…are much less in price."* (1884).[547]

On behalf of the Ekegren watch, one dealer boasted: *"The finest and most accurate timepiece that can be produced by human skill."* (1889).[548]

Another wrote: *"Incomparably the finest high-grade timekeeper in existence."* (1887).[549]

Finally, on behalf of some of the leading luxury Swiss producers: *"The Ekegren Watch, The Audemars Watch, The Vacheron and Constantin Watch…The most accurate timekeepers known."* (1888).[550]

'Finesse' and 'accuracy' were the Swiss descriptors, compared to Waltham's claims of 'cheap' and 'reliable.'

What was, perhaps, so noteworthy about the Swiss' focus on the global luxury market was the foresight that enough wealthy individuals would want luxury watches over mass-produced cheap and reliable watches. The story from the Centennial Exhibition had been the precision of machine-made watches and the wide popularity of cheap but reliable Waltham watches. However, as the wealthy upper class gained enormous amounts of money in the Gilded Age (the top 1% owned 45% of the wealth by 1900),[551] the phenomenon of conspicuous consumption led the wealthy few to want what others could not afford.

It would have been out of style to display wealth as a symbol of status. Instead, Victorian values promoted progress; displaying wealth as a symbol of progress was acceptable. Technology was a symbol of advancement, so owning a machine-made watch (now made by both the Swiss and Americans) was progressive itself; [552] a very complicated or intricate luxury machine-made watch was the ultimate symbol. Those who could not afford the real thing wanted as close to it as possible. American economist Thorstein Veblen, who coined the term "conspicuous consumption," correctly identified the Gilded Age consumers' willingness to purchase even counterfeit goods in an effort to appear wealthy.[553]

The Swiss implicitly understood the concept of conspicuous consumption and executed their strategy precisely at the right time. By 1880, the economy was recovering from the Panic of 1873 and Gilded Age wealth began to grow quickly among a few wealthy consumers. Society became increasingly consumption-focused.

Veblen's famous work *The Theory of the Leisure Class,* written in 1899 noted the tendency for consumers to spend seemingly inexplicable premiums for the finest items. This included specialized products whose utility far exceeded the average customer's needs, such as calendar and repeater watches. He wrote: "The quasi-peaceable gentleman of leisure, then, not only consumes of the staff of life beyond the minimum required for subsistence and physical efficiency, but his consumption also undergoes a specialisation as regards the quality of the goods consumed. He consumes freely and of the best, in…ornaments, apparel… accoutrements, amusements, amulets, and idols or divinities."[554]

He also seemed to characterize the Swiss penchant for innovating increasingly complex watch movements that most certainly exceeded the need of any human being, but were resolute in their superiority for craftsmanship: "the motive principle and the proximate aim of innovation is no doubt the higher efficiency of the improved and more elaborate products for personal comfort and well-being."[555]

At its core, the watch was a fashion accessory. The watch chain was draped across the owner's belly, connected to the hidden watch that was an often-checked symbol of one's status. The owner had to withdraw it from their pocket to observe the time; the motion itself was a sign of moderate status. A bright gold watch would have been easily recognized whenever one was asked for the time or when checked in a public place, as if announcing the owner's position in society.[556]

As historian Michael O'Malley observed, "Tucked into the bulging vest of newspaper-cartoon capitalists, the gold watch helped symbolize the Gilded Age plutocrat."[557] Veblen adequately summarized why the expensive, luxury Swiss pocket watch, usually carried in the vest pocket, appealed to the wealthy, fashionable consumer:

> *expenditure on dress has this advantage over most other methods, that our apparel is always in evidence and affords an indication*

of our pecuniary standing to all observers at the first glance...It is true of dress in even a higher degree than of most other items of consumption, that people will undergo a very considerable degree of privation in the comforts or the necessaries of life in order to afford what is considered a decent amount of wasteful consumption.[558]

A second reason the best Swiss producers continued to be perceived as luxury watchmakers was the sheer differences in volume and subsequent exclusivity of the product. Waltham's watches were produced in the hundreds of thousands of units per year, increasing to a million per year by the beginning of the twentieth century. Waltham never attempted scarcity; it did just the opposite. Meanwhile, the most notable Swiss luxury makers produced only tens to a few thousand watches each year, with some watches requiring multiple years of labor to produce.

Most cheap Swiss watches of the era were mass-produced like Waltham, but the best brands of the Swiss hierarchy provided an elitist opportunity for the Gilded Age's wealthy class to own something that few others had or could afford. Thus, Waltham provided a watch that most customers could afford while the luxury Swiss producers manufactured a limited quantity that many consumers *aspired* to afford.

American Consul-to-Switzerland Samuel Byers also warned Americans of the quickly diminishing reputation of Waltham compared to its Swiss competitors. His warning made its way into American newspapers: "[Byers] says that almost every American tourist carries home from Switzerland a good Swiss watch...at [the Melbourne] exhibition there were some very good Swiss watches and no very good Waltham watches."[559]

This change in perception was exemplified in an 1892 article published in the *Brooklyn Daily Eagle* on page two, which documented the watches owned and worn by over 200 wealthy individuals. It occupied five of eight columns on the page and told readers what their senators, mayor, county officials, professors, reverends, doctors, and businessmen wore for their watch. It was effectively a "who's who" of Brooklyn.

The importance of placement of this article indicated that readers cared about the watches people wore. It also revealed which watches were owned by wealthy American consumers. A majority of those were Swiss (39%), followed by American (23%) and English (22%) production. When looking at the reported values of those watches, Swiss watches accounted for 44% of the value as opposed to American watches, which were 19% of the reported value demonstrating the Swiss watches were, on average, far more expensive and valuable. The reader of the paper would have seen that the mayor, senators, judges, and many of the reported important wealthy individuals of Brooklyn owned expensive Swiss watches made by Matile, Jürgensen, Ekegren, and Patek Phillipe.[560]

Congress even attempted to further stifle Swiss competition through more-aggressive tariffs. In 1897, the United States congress enacted the Dingley Tariff, which placed a drastic increase in taxes on goods imported into America. The American watch industry was one of the major proponents of the new law.[561] Despite the tariff, the American government was surprised to note that Americans *increased* their importation of expensive Swiss watches. The

193

government reported that, "The increase…is almost entirely in high-grade watches and movements, and is not only gratifying but surprising to the Geneva makers, who expected to see their business with the United States largely decreased rather than increased after the passage of the present tariff bill."[562] As American and European prosperity increased, so too did the world's demand for luxury Swiss watches.

By 1899, the U.S. only accounted for 1.5% of Swiss luxury sales. The luxury Swiss watchmakers exported 3,997 watches to the United States.[563] In that same year, Waltham only produced 230 luxury watches of 515,500 total watches.[564] The United States was not Switzerland's largest market for luxury watches either. The U.S. was the seventh-largest market for luxury watches, well behind Germany (28%) and Great Britain (19%).[565] Worldwide, the Swiss exported 329,000 luxury watches alone and over three million total watches.[566]

By 1890, an American newspaper admitted that a "much smaller number of high priced watches made in Switzerland show much larger financial returns in proportion to the total number made than in America, where the majority are extremely low priced."[567] The Swiss monopoly on expensive watches led to profits, not just in America, but across the world. In Brazil, it was said that "no one doubts the quality of high-grade Swiss watches, and since they are usually cheaper in price than the American high-grade watches, [the latter] are at a serious disadvantage."[568] From 1885 to 1900, Swiss luxury watch sales comprised 40% of the total value sold.[569]

Waltham's well-earned reputation for making high-performing luxury watches at the Centennial, and later, high-grade railroad watches, never brought

194

Waltham a stronger position in the market when compared to the Swiss. For Waltham, luxury manufacture of the *AWC* grade or other similar luxury models comprised one percent of Waltham's production from 1885 to 1900. Meanwhile, cheaper watches that sold for less than $30 were 80% of its production.[570]

In early 1884, while the Swiss were finding notable success, Robbins reinforced the Waltham strategy towards cheap and reliable:

> *All [our] cheaper goods sell readily. It is only the higher grades which hang heavy on our hands. Unfortunately it is just those on which we make most profit...we have decided to curtail considerably the manufacture of the finer classes of goods. It certainly is not good policy to go on piling up stock which the market is not ready for. We are consequently turning our force upon the cheaper grades, which for the present are most in demand.*[571]

Time on one's wrist

While these strategic maneuvers were occurring across the global markets in the 1880s and 1890s, it would be Waltham's reluctance to embrace the wristwatch phenomenon taking hold that became its most iconic folly. The Swiss watchmakers generally introduced the wristwatch in the 1880s for the military, though the concept of putting a watch on the wrist was nothing novel.

Its utility caught public attention during the Boer War (1899 to 1902), and by World War I, the Swiss were known for their production of smaller wrist watches. It required innovation to produce a mechanical movement so small that it could comfortably fit on the wrist and survive the shocks of hand movements and bumps.[572] Hans Wilsdorf, the founder of Rolex, was one of the first to see the mass market potential of the wristwatch and committed the company entirely to this risky new product.

During their journey of transformation, the Swiss watchmakers were in search of new markets and products, which led to experimentation and innovation with wristwatches. They had no sunk costs in factory machinery since they were only starting to transition to a mechanized system, making the move to the wristwatch easier. Even once the Swiss had many machines, they were designed to allow flexibility in production, though they also required a more skilled operator. What was an even more significant benefit was that many Swiss producers only focused on making components rather than full watches, creating a nimbler system of subcontracting that could quickly adapt to new consumer demands without incurring substantial sunk costs to any individual factory.[573]

The modular system provided another advantage as well: when one Swiss inventor developed a new watch component, it could be used by multiple watchmakers through the network of contracting. Therefore, many Swiss watchmakers could integrate the latest innovations into their designs. Economist Richard Langlois noted that this allowed "the Swiss manufacturers [to] set the pace in catering to [the wristwatch] market, and domestic producers [such as Waltham] followed as best they could."[574]

The wristwatch was a symbol of Swiss assimilation of market trends, while Waltham was firmly stuck in the production of pocket watches and failed to adapt at the discretion of its managers. By the late 1880s, Fitch had already implemented policies that began to stifle the innovative culture, focusing entirely on cost reduction. Concerning transitioning to wristwatch production, it was noted that: "there was a serious shortage of skilled watch designers and toolmakers [at Waltham]. It was even questioned whether Americans could compete with Swiss skill on such fine, delicate work as the new [wristwatch] designs required."[575]

This was a remarkable turn of events for the company that previously invented so quickly and with such finesse that the skilled watchmakers of Switzerland had found themselves in an existential crisis in 1876 and looked to Waltham as a model. The wristwatch was an embodiment of the strategic managers' failure to adapt Waltham's asset-heavy structure as the market became further commoditized.

The company had no financial freedom of maneuver in its cost structure to allow it to move to revolutionary new products like the wristwatch. It took Waltham until the 1920s to firmly commit to wristwatches, but by this time, the Swiss were already known around the world for their products and had regained all the market share they had lost during Waltham's rise.[576] The Swiss dominance of the wristwatch was rewarding, considering 50% of early wristwatches would be regarded as luxury products made with gold or platinum, capturing enormous profit margins for the Swiss.[577]

The Waltham management of the 1860s and 1870s probably would have embraced the wristwatch change, if not identified the consumer demand and been

197

a first mover. But not the Waltham of 1885 to 1900. By this time, the company was solely focused on remaining profitable in the low-cost market, which was only possible by being able to produce at the smallest per-unit cost.

The myopia of finding greater economies of scale was captured in one of Robbins' reports to shareholders. In almost-consecutive sentences, he declared that the company's sales revenue increased 40% yet profits increased only 1 to 2%, while in the same year the company invested heavily in machinery to make the watch *even cheaper*, while also mentioning that Waltham had the reputation for *making the cheapest watch already*.[578] It was a seriously written, yet almost farcical series of statements, describing a company chasing an outcome and never catching it due to severe competition in a commoditized market of low-grade watches.

The chase did not relent for decades. It was a marked contrast from the Swiss, who over the same period, managed to earn prestige for making premium and innovative watches even though there was no noticeable performance gap in timekeeping between higher-grade Waltham and Swiss watches during the era.

Waltham's regression

The strategic devolution of Waltham over the years following the Panic of 1873 and the Centennial Exhibition was significant and can be seen using some simple financial performance ratios used in modern business analysis. The Panic of 1873 had a notable effect on Waltham, but when looking past the critical years of

1873 to 1877, it becomes obvious that the combined effect of strategic choices, intense competition, and a recovering Swiss industry led to Waltham's devolving position. From a strategic perspective, the Swiss cut off Waltham's ability to gain sales overseas as well as any chance Waltham could have had to gain luxury sales. Meanwhile, competition eroded any competitive advantage it once held in low-cost watches.

In business, a company theoretically invests in assets where it thinks it will get the most benefit when factoring in the opportunity cost of using the money elsewhere. A way of measuring the return on investments such as machinery is performed by looking at the profits compared to total assets, known as Return on Assets (ROA) in the modern era.[579] ROA is considered "the most effective, broadly available financial measure to assess company performance. It captures the fundamentals of business performance in a holistic way."[580] When profits do not grow despite investments in new machinery, factory, and production, "the decline signals companies' decreasing ability to find and capture attractive opportunities relative to the assets they have."[581]

In the years immediately following the Civil War, Waltham consistently maintained a ROA above 12%. Early signs of a diminishing competitive advantage could be seen around 1867 when the Civil War ended, and Elgin was in full operation (see chart below). A debilitating and permanent slide began after Fitch took over as superintendent in 1883. Waltham continued to invest in assets with the hope that it could return to its competitive cost advantage.[582] These investments resulted in significant capital expenditures with negligible gains in efficiency and no improvement to profits. The company's ROA permanently dropped below 6% by 1892, never to return above before 1900.

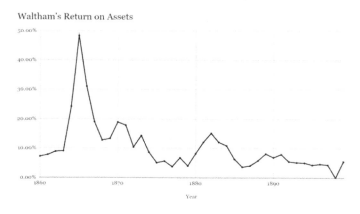

Waltham's Return on Assets

Calculated by dividing annual profits by annual assets. Based on Waltham's annual reports to shareholders. (Calculated by the author)

Waltham's chase after low-cost competitors instead of making serious efforts to move upmarket towards luxury sales must have stunned the Swiss, who watched Waltham achieve a reputational victory at the Centennial for making the best luxury watches in the world. The luxury Swiss producers did not ever have to face Waltham directly.

The changing of the guard was evident by the 1893 Columbian Exhibition in Chicago. It served as a symbolic marker of change for both Waltham and the Swiss. It emphasized the Swiss' advance and Waltham's retreat.

The 1893 Columbian Exhibition

At The 1893 Columbian Exhibition, Waltham repeated its earlier performance from the 1876 Centennial, except on a much grander scale. This time,

200

Waltham brought near-fully automatic machinery, where it was claimed that: "one operative, with a set of this machinery, can do as much work as twenty operatives could do...at the time of the Centennial in 1876."[583] Yet, Waltham appeared to have no idea about its precarious situation at the hands of the Swiss, who had made great strides in the previous seventeen years.

Going into the Columbian Exhibition, one senior Waltham manager told a reporter that the Swiss and other foreign makers "had been out of business [for] several years."[584] This was not true and it was impossible that the manager believed this, but it demonstrated something about Waltham: the company never strategically embraced that the Swiss could present a legitimate competitive threat. At the Columbian Exhibition, everyone else would realize Waltham's ignorance.

The Swiss learned from their mistake at the 1876 Centennial and this time they brought three large exhibits for watches. The first was an entire area devoted to the famous luxury maker Patek, Philippe, & Co. A second area was for the luxury producers of Geneva, and a third was bestowed upon the mountain watchmakers of the Jura region.[585] The judges were impressed with the Swiss watches, where they noted the Swiss hybrid system of factory production: "The use of machinery in making interchangeable and other parts is carried as far as possible, and the most skilled artists are secured to fill the various positions of adjusting, escapement making, jeweling, engraving, enamel painting, case making, and all the other departments where great personal ability is required."[586] In other words, the Swiss were successful in using mass production but preserved the best aspects of Swiss artisanal skill.

In noting the accomplishments of Patek, Philippe, & Co, the judges lauded its use of machines, writing that machine work, "combined with the best principles of construction, great attention to details, high finish, and accurate performance, has given this firm a richly deserved and world-wide reputation."[587]

The judges' report from this world's fair provided a marked contrast from 1876. Various comments praised the reformed Swiss industry:

> *While looking over the [Swiss] exhibits we were so impressed with their magnificence, artistic beauty, and great mechanical skill shown, that only an attempt can be made in stereotyped expressions to give some idea of them, for they baffle description...Great attention is given to the accurate performance of their watches, many of them being rated and tested before being sent out to compete with watches of other makers at the various trials at the observatories.*[588]

Sources of the Swiss resurgence and success

The judges determined that a few specific factors deserved credit for the remarkable Swiss transformation, many of which could be traced back to the recommendations contained in David's report. The judges rhetorically asked: "In regard to their immense progress in the past fifteen years, it will be inquired, how has it been accomplished?"

The principal sources of success were the "Nine watchmaking schools, supplied with the latest chronometrical and mechanical improvements under the teaching of their most expert masters, contribute to the present reputation of their productions."[589] David was the most ardent advocate for these changes to the watchmaking curriculum in Switzerland, beginning with the school in St. Imier. By 1893, all of the major watchmaking schools in Switzerland were integrating the new mechanical methods of watchmaking and instructing their students in the hybrid system.[590] The modernized curriculum notably impressed the judges.

Then there was David's suggested emphasis on quality control of Swiss products. The judges reported that: "no watch can obtain a certificate unless it faithfully performs in all the stipulated conditions [of testing]."[591] Yet, the Swiss had managed to make the certified and adjusted watch much more accessible to consumers: "It is somewhat a novelty to see a watch selling at a moderate price accompanied by an observatory certificate, but here we had them in abundance."[592]

Finally, David's call for a collective response, though not universally accepted, was a success for production syndication and promoting industry innovation and advancement. The judges said that the Swiss' cooperation resulted in a narrative that was markedly different from the cutthroat practices stemming from the Waltham/Elgin rivalry. The judges reported that the Swiss' "horological societies are very active, always discussing and examining any new improvements in the construction of watches, and receive the aid of their commercial and scientific institutions and periodical publications, all combining to advance and perfect their knowledge in this art."[593]

Waltham proves it lost its edge

In sharp contrast, Waltham's performance at the Columbian Exhibition was a metaphor for the company's trajectory since Philadelphia. The judges noted the elaborate, expensive exhibit, complete with $15,000 in wood paneling.[594] The exhibit's fully automatic machinery emphasized the company's continuous movement towards more efficient production at a great cost. At this fair, Waltham displayed 2,000 watches, which were the production of *one day* instead of the 1876 Centennial's 2,200 watch exhibit showing *one week's* worth of production. It once again demonstrated strategic management devoid of innovative ideas, simply using what had worked before, but with no ability to capture imaginations as Waltham had done seventeen years prior.

The judges did not note any performance characteristics of Waltham's watches. Every comment about Waltham related to its impressive exhibit and machinery, while there was not a single report of the company providing superior or notable performance in watchmaking. Meanwhile, the judges wrote twenty-two pages about the amazing performance of Swiss watches and the sources of their remarkable recovery, including seven pages devoted to the watchmaking schools' curriculum. It was quite a different story than the Centennial Exhibition.[595]

This time, Elgin chose to stay away from the world's fair, even though it was taking place near its hometown. Elgin's shareholders deemed it not worth the expenditure.[596] According to one newspaper report, Waltham and Elgin had both agreed to not participate, but Waltham began preparations for an exhibit anyway. Elgin did not find out until it was too late.[597] If this was true, it was a reflection of the American competitive landscape.

After the completion of the world's fair, Robbins wrote to shareholders, as if writing a summary of Waltham's performance over the last fifteen years: "It ended for us…in a total loss of all we expended upon it…No profits from it are yet perceived."[598] It was just like Waltham's many investments through the years: a display of immense mass production that ended in no greater profits.

Chapter 15:

Espionage, Strategic Divergence, and Consequences

A Waltham porcelain dial circa 1877 (Author's photo)

"...it seems opportune to recapitulate for your information the facts of our total manufacture, our sales and our profits."

-Royal Robbins, *1894 Annual Report to Shareholders*

Looking Back – 2022

      A widely circulated 1907 Waltham advertisement summarized the reversal of fortunes experienced over the previous three decades, emphasizing how far one had fallen and the other had risen. The ad pleaded: "Who [tries] to keep alive the notion that the Swiss watch is better than the American watch? Those dealers who recommend Swiss watches, not because of higher quality, but because of higher profit. Waltham watches are the best in the world."[599]

The advertisement was hardly an improvement over a street hawker attempting to sell a dubious product. Thirty years prior, the underlying premise of the advertisement was unthinkable. Yet after three decades of chasing lower costs and cheaper products, Waltham found its reputation vastly diminished. What once seemed like inevitable global domination of the watch industry had turned into a low-profit, commoditized production with no residual recognition for excellence. Meanwhile, the formerly 'defeated' mountain watchmakers were recognized for quality across the globe.

Did David's actions matter?

The 1876 Centennial Exhibition led to a series of actions that ultimately changed the tide of industrial combat in the watch industry. Most conspicuously, it highlights the risk that inadequate trade secrecy poses. It was a risk that Robbins himself came to recognize when he felt the need to re-justify his decision to show the machines at the Centennial. In 1878, he told shareholders that the exhibit had provoked competitors and "given our rivals some new weapons of attack," but he was still "entirely satisfied" with the outcome.[600] A year later, in 1879, he told shareholders that they should not expect him to share strategic plans for production as "It would not be prudent as respects our competitors who, as it is, in some way learn them earlier than they should."[601] In 1881, he prefaced his strategic plans by telling investors: "Without detailing our plans for the future or giving our reasons for them to an imprudent extent which I am sure you will not wish me to do..."[602]

Had Robbins realized what David had done? If so, he never indicated this was the source, yet modern analyses of industrial espionage show that the victim often avoids admitting the problematic and embarrassing reality.[603]

The Swiss watchmakers thought the information David had acquired to be so important that the SIIJ created a committee in 1877 whose charge was to gather information about international competitors, with the main focus being Waltham. In 1887, this turned into an organized business intelligence unit. By this action alone, the Swiss demonstrated that they found David's gathered intelligence to be critical to the Swiss' survival and an effort worth continuing.[604]

Yet the outcomes of this story reach much deeper than stolen trade secrets or the risk of espionage. David's espionage only explains how the Swiss acquired information but does not account for what they were able to do with it. The information David acquired was only interesting data without David distilling its implications and possibilities. He was effective because he knew what to do with the information, which is often the critical missing link between raw intelligence and proper tactical, operational, and strategic action.

David's vision and leadership were seen in the industrial combat and the divergence between the Swiss and their powerful American counterpart. Horology historian Richard Watkins, writing on the enduring significance of David's report, wrote: "My admiration for David stems from his ten recommendations... This list encompasses nearly all of the main developments in Switzerland from 1877 onwards, and it doesn't include David's probable influence on industrial organisation."[605]

Historian Jean-Marc Barrelet would give primary credit to David: "Jacques David, Théodore Gribi and the others were the principal agents for the modernization of the Swiss watch industry. With courage and perseverance, they convinced the recalcitrant of the need for progress and mechanization. Beyond the simple use of machines, which everyone already understood, it was necessary to persuade the watchmaking world to move from the bench into the factory."[606]

Accordingly, the Swiss showed that emulation of production methods leveled the field. But more importantly, they demonstrated that a sound strategy of moving into growing markets and out of declining ones was far superior to Waltham's impressive economies of scale. Business historian Alfred Chandler summarized the benefits of the Swiss strategy:

> [The most effective firms] no longer competed on the basis of price. Instead they competed for market share and profits through functional and strategic effectiveness. They did so functionally by improving their product, their processes of production, their marketing, their purchasing, and their labor relations, and strategically by moving into growing markets more rapidly, and out of declining ones more quickly and effectively, than did their competitors.[607]

The core reason for Waltham's failure

At Waltham, it was Robbins and then Fitch executing the same time-tested strategy that failed to adapt and resulted in the company's eventual troubles. Waltham's senior managers remained committed to the low-cost strategy even as competition meant it was untenable. Even in 1921, George Blow's study of Waltham showed that the chase after 'cheap and reliable' never stopped: "Under the keen competition which exists today in a buyer's market, it is necessary to sell things at a lower price than heretofore. The cost of production therefore, is now, more than ever before, an element of most vital importance."[608]

In a *Harvard Business Review* article titled "Why good companies go bad," the author summarized the condition from which Waltham succumbed:

> *The problem is not an inability to take action but an inability to take appropriate action. There can be many reasons for the problem — ranging from managerial stubbornness to sheer incompetence — but one of the most common is a condition that I call active inertia...Active inertia is an organization's tendency to follow established patterns of behavior — even in response to dramatic environmental shifts. Stuck in the modes of thinking and working that brought success in the past, market leaders simply accelerate all their tried-and-true activities. In trying to dig themselves out of a hole, they just deepen it.* [609]

The direct source of Waltham's failure was its management, but more specifically, the refusal to adapt the company's strategy in a quickly changing global

211

market between 1876 and 1900. The confluence of Waltham's flawed strategies acting in concert with the adapting Swiss industry overwhelmed Waltham.

The effect of espionage on Waltham's downfall

The American watch industry's experience is a common outcome of industrial espionage; rarely does the theft of trade secrets directly lead to the downfall of a competitor in the short term. Instead, the stolen secrets inform future actions and dictate strategic moves and investments that degrade a competitor's advantage over years or decades.

During the passage of the 1996 Industrial Espionage Act, the U.S. Government's report noted the often-intangible value of information acquired through espionage: "a piece of information can be as valuable as a factory is to a business. The theft of that information can do more harm than if an arsonist torched that factory."[610]

A more recent study demonstrated this concept in the aggregate. Looking at industrial espionage in former East and West Germany, the authors found that espionage had a significant effect over decades and that the economic productivity gap between East and West would have been significant without the East stealing trade secrets from companies in the West. The researchers concluded: "Our results provide evidence of significant economic returns to industrial espionage."[611]

In the report on the Industrial Espionage Act, the U.S. Senate further explained why the managerial and process information acquired by David was so valuable to the Swiss and conversely, harmful to Waltham. The Senate wrote:

> *The value of [proprietary information] is almost entirely dependent on its being a closely held secret. It includes, but is not limited to, information such as production processes, bid estimates, production schedules, computer software, technology schematics, and trade secrets. It is, in short, the very information that drives the American economy. For many companies this information is the keystone to their economic competitiveness. They spend many millions of dollars developing the information, take great pains and invest enormous resources to keep it secret, and expect to reap rewards from their investment.*[612]

What if?

The net effect of David's espionage can best be evaluated by asking oneself what would have happened if David had *not* visited Waltham and the other American factories? *Not* acquired any proprietary information? *Not* written the report? And *not* contributed his insights and leadership?

Perhaps the Swiss would have eventually transformed and adapted to the changing market conditions anyway. But what if the Swiss had not reformed, rather they continued to fade as watchmakers much like the English, French, and Germans had done before them?

The history of Waltham would have proceeded with very different conclusions and America might have endured as the world's best watchmakers under a different competitive landscape. But this did not happen, and the fact remains that the Swiss unquestionably remain the world's best watchmakers over 140 years later.

Waltham's terminal decline

During Ezra Fitch's tenure spanning 1883 to 1921, the company made irreversible decisions including its cuts to innovation and massive investments in operating assets. As Fitch's role in the company rose, Robbins' declined both physically and emotionally. His last report to shareholders was officially in 1894, but by this point, his letters were simple reports of perfunctory business, no longer demonstrating command of the industry. Yet, Fitch did not have control of the shareholders nor their confidence and they often interfered with his management of the company: "Fitch was the titular head of a system rather than a dominant leader...under his regime the old forms of management were preserved, but substance of authority had departed...There was no force in the company strong enough to drive it in a new direction."[613] Rather than focusing on making their products better, Waltham worried about staying profitable and resorted to collusion and price-fixing.

Fitch regularly corresponded with Charles Hulburd, the president of Elgin while colluding on prices in violation of the Sherman Anti-Trust Act (1890) which prohibited anti-competitive agreements and horizontal price-fixing between competitors.[614] Both companies understood what they were doing was illegal, but they had departed from efforts to make a better product to overcome competition and instead relied on anti-competitive tactics. In a 1905 letter between Elgin, Waltham, and another watchcase company, Elgin's Hulburd wrote: "Now there is not a particle of evidence which they could get to prove this [collusion], unless we make admissions ourselves."[615]

Waltham's focus on reducing competition and covering up the agreements rather than on product innovation contributed to its long-term demise. Meanwhile, the much more inventive Swiss watchmakers led the global markets in reputation with their new products, including the wristwatch. It is noteworthy that in 1905, the same year this letter was written, Hans Wilsdorf, the founder of Rolex, began his work.

Waltham eventually failed as a company after a series of poor strategic choices and a long terminal decline. It survived until 1923 when it was forced to restructure, then again until 1948 when it filed for bankruptcy and conducted another series of reorganizations, but it was not a significant strategic concern in the global watch market beyond 1900.

In a historical sense, Waltham failed so remarkably that most people have no idea that America ever had a watch industry, much less an innovative, dominant, and progressive company. Meanwhile, the luxury Swiss watch is one of the most regionally associated products in modern history. It was the disparate mountain watchmakers, who put together such an effective response to the American onslaught that they wiped American watchmaking from the map and living memory.

Bally had identified what was happening in 1876, calling it "combat of industry."

A battle it was, and the Swiss were victorious.

Endnotes:

[1] "Definition of Disrupt," Merriam Webster Dictionary, 2018, https://www.merriam-webster.com/dictionary/disrupt.

[2] John Swinton, "A Model Factory in a Model City: A Social Study of the Waltham Watch Factory" (New York, 1887), 5, Hathitrust, http://hdl.handle.net/2027/hvd.32044013681051.

[3] "The Watch as a Growth Industry," *Appleton's Journal: Literature, Science, and Art*, July 9, 1870, 36.

[4] See Jacques David, *American and Swiss Watchmaking in 1876*, trans. Richard Watkins (Kingston, Tasmania: Richard Watkins, 2003), http://www.watkinsr.id.au/. for the translation I read.

[5] Kathryn L. MacKay, "Notable Labor Strikes of the Gilded Age," accessed October 14, 2018, http://faculty.weber.edu/kmackay/notable_labor_strikes_of_the_gil.htm.

[6] The earliest known reference to the report in academic literature was a Swiss academic article written in 1987, over 100 years after the original report was written and published by Jacques David. The citation said the report was kept in the archives of Neuchatel. However, in my efforts to determine exactly when this report made its way to the public archives, I was referred to Longines' 1992 facsimile edition. Despite repeated attempts to determine *exactly* when the David report became publicly available, I was unsuccessful.

[7] See Alexis McCrossen, *Marking Modern Times: A History of Clocks, Watches, and Other Timekeepers in American Life* (Chicago: The University of Chicago Press, 2013), n. 47. where McCrossen references David's report for further reading.

[8] Jean-Marc Barrelet, "Les Résistances à l'innovation Dans l'industrie Horlogère Des Montagnes Neuchâteloises à La Fin Du XIXe Siècle," *Swiss Journal of History* 37 (1987): 398.This casual translation was performed using Google Translate.

[9] Edward Bally and Edward Dubied, *Industry and Manufactures in the United States: Look Out for Yourselves!* (Boston: Beacon Press, 1878), 5.

[10] David, *American and Swiss Watchmaking in 1876*, 82.

[11] Royal E. Robbins, "Treasurer's Report, 1879, American (Waltham) Watch Company," Annual Report to Shareholders (Waltham Watch Company, 1879), Vol. AD-2, Special Collections, Baker Library, Harvard Business School.

[12] I thank the anonymous reviewer who succinctly pointed out this conclusion.

[13] Lewis Mumford, *Technics and Civilization* (University of Chicago Press, 2010), 15.

[14] Mumford, 14.

[15] Alexander Graham Bell, "Letter from Alexander Graham Bell to Mabel Hubbard Bell, June 21, 1876," June 21, 1876, 21, Library of Congress, https://www.loc.gov/resource/magbell.03500116/?sp=17&st=text.

[16] James D. McCabe, *The Illustrated History of the Centennial Exhibition* (National Publishing Company, 1876), 848–49.

[17] McCabe, 852.

[18] McCabe, 340–41.

[19] McCabe, 333.

[20] McCabe, 295.

[21] McCabe, 339–40.

[22] McCabe, 280.

[23] "Going to the Centennial: A Guy to the Exhibition," 22.

[24] "Centennial Jottings No. 3," *Lowell Daily Citizen*, June 29, 1876.

[25] See Edouard Favre-Perret, "Watchmaking in America: A Foreigner's Testimony," in *Report from the International Exhibition at Philadelphia* (New York: Robbins & Appleton, 1877), 31 for Swiss export statistics summary.

[26] C.E. DeLong, "Memories of America's Noted Horologist: Theophilus Gribi," *Horology*, June 1937, 34–36.

[27] There is a discrepancy between Gribi's calculation and reality. The machine operated between 5-7 seconds per cycle, which produces around 8,000 screws a day, which is about 2,000 less than Gribi's calculation. Regardless of the exact amount, it was significant.

[28] Theophilus Gribi, "1876 Worlds Fair Notes on Watch Exhibits - All Countries, Theo. Gribi - Swiss Commissioner [Photo Copy of Original]" (1876), Private Collection.

[29] Oliver Harper, "Waltham Watch Company," *Daily Alta California and San Francisco Times*, August 27, 1876.

[30] Donald R. Hoke, *Ingenious Yankees: The Rise of the American Manufactures in the Private Sector* (New York: Columbia University Press, 1990), 208. Thank you to collector George Collord for hosting me, showing me one of these machines in operation, and telling me all about them.

[31] See "Pay Roll, American (Waltham) Watch Company" (Waltham Watch Company Records, November 1876), sec. July, Vol. KC-10, Baker Library Special Collections, Harvard Business School which lists Waltham's Centennial employees.

[32] McCabe, *The Illustrated History of the Centennial Exhibition*, 281.

[33] "Going to the Centennial: A Guy to the Exhibition," 25–26.

[34] Royal E. Robbins, "Treasurer's Report, 1876, American (Waltham) Watch Company," Annual Report to Shareholders (Waltham Watch Company, 1876), 8, Vol. AD-1, Special Collections, Baker Library, Harvard Business School; interested readers can find the transcripts of Waltham's annual reports from 1859 to 1899 available from the National Association of Watch and Clock Collector's Lending Library. Vernon M. Hawkins, ed., *The American Watch Company Annual Reports to Stockholders 1859 - 1899 [Transcribed from Original Company Records]* (West Boxford, MA: Self-published, 1984).

[35] Robbins, "Treasurer's Report, 1876, American (Waltham) Watch Company," 8.

[36] See "Official Register of Directors and Officers of the Union Pacific Railroad Company and the Union Pacific Railway Company, 1863-1889" (Union Pacific Railroad Company, 1890), 7–8, http://hdl.handle.net/2027/uc2.ark:/13960/t9862f20v.

[37] Robbins, "Treasurer's Report, 1876, American (Waltham) Watch Company," 8.

[38] Leslie Nesky, ed., "Waltham Free Press, 16 June 1876 in 'The American Watch Company 1876,'" *National Association of Watch and Clock Collectors' Bulletin*, The American Watch Company 1876, April 2004, 165.

[39] *American and Swiss Watchmaking in 1876*, sec. Gribi Letter (Preface).

[40] Bally and Dubied, *Industry and Manufactures in the United States: Look Out for Yourselves!*, 14.

[41] Bally and Dubied, viii.

[42] Bally and Dubied, 21.

[43] Bally and Dubied, sec. Translator's Note (viii).

[44] Bally and Dubied, 5–6.

[45] Bally and Dubied, 5.

[46] Ronald C. White, *American Ulysses: A Life of Ulysses S. Grant* (Random House Publishing Group, 2017), 220.

[47] Thank you to Dr. Alexis McCrossen for her discussion with the author on this point.

[48] McCrossen, *Marking Modern Times*, 64.

[49] Michael O'Malley, *Keeping Watch: A History of American Time* (New York: Viking, 1990), 151–52.

[50] "The Watch as a Growth Industry," 30–31.

[51] O'Malley, *Keeping Watch: A History of American Time*, 147.

[52] Thank you to Clint Geller and Alexis McCrossen for their discussion with the author on this point.

[53] Author's calculations based on US adult population, watch production, and watch imports

[54] "The Watch as a Growth Industry," 31.

[55] "Watchmaking by Machinery," *Chambers's Journal of Popular Literature, Arts, and Sciences* 4, no. 680 (1877): 93.

[56] "The Watch as a Growth Industry," 31.

[57] Favre-Perret, "Watchmaking in America: A Foreigner's Testimony," 32.

[58] Favre-Perret, 31.

[59] Favre-Perret, 33.

[60] McCabe, *The Illustrated History of the Centennial Exhibition*, 448.

[61] Favre-Perret, "Watchmaking in America: A Foreigner's Testimony," 31.

[62] Jacques David, "Letter from Jacques David to Ernest Francillon, September 1876," in *Longines, from a Family Business to a Global Brand*, by Pierre-Yves Donzé, trans. Rosamund Bandi-Tebbut (St. Imeir: Editions des Longines, 2012).

[63] David, *American and Swiss Watchmaking in 1876*, sec. Gribi's Letter (preface).

[64] David, sec. Preface (pg 6).

[65] David, sec. Preface (p. 6).

[66] "Passenger List: S.S. Amerique, 23 Aug 1876" (U.S. Government, August 23, 1876), New York Passenger Lists 1820-1891.

[67] David is the only one for which there is evidence he entered Waltham's factory (as he admitted it in a letter). However, Gribi was his partner in all respects. David even references "us" in his letter and reports. Both were commissioned by the SIIJ and Gribi is considered by most to also be represented by David's report, which was the product of espionage.

[68] "The Watch as a Growth Industry," 32.

[69] Philip T. Priestley, *Aaron Lufkin Dennison: An Industrial Pioneer and His Legacy* (Columbia, PA: National Association of Watch & Clock Collectors, Inc., 2009), 10.

[70] Charles W. Moore, *Timing a Century: History of the Waltham Watch Company*, Harvard Studies in Business History (Cambridge, Mass.: Harvard University Press, 1945), 9.

[71] Landes, *Revolution in Time*, 311.

[72] Landes, 311.

[73] Landes, 313.

[74] Richard Watkins, *Watchmaking and the American System of Manufacturing (Revised)* (Kingston, Tasmania: Richard Watkins, 2009), 34–35.

[75] See Royal E. Robbins, "Treasurer's Report, 1870, American (Waltham) Watch Company," Annual Report to Shareholders (Waltham Watch Company, 1870), 5, Vol. AD-1, Special Collections, Baker Library, Harvard Business School.

[76] Watkins, *Watchmaking and the American System of Manufacturing (Revised)*; Moore, *Timing a Century: History of the Waltham Watch Company*, 232.

[77] Moore, *Timing a Century: History of the Waltham Watch Company*, 14, 19, 243–44.

[78] William H. Keith, *A Family Tale or History of American Watchmaking in Five Chapters (1883)*, ed. Richard Watkins (Kingston, Tasmania: Richard Watkins, 2007), 65.

[79] Charles W. Moore, *Timing a Century: History of the Waltham Watch Company*, Harvard Studies in Business History (Cambridge, Mass.: Harvard University Press, 1945), 19, 243–44.

[80] Michael C. Harrold, "Fulfillment of American Industrial Watch Manufacture: Royal Robbins Launches the Waltham Watch," *National Association of Watch and Clock Collectors' Bulletin*, October 1999, 581.

[81] Robbins, "Treasurer's Report, 1870, American (Waltham) Watch Company," 5.

[82] Harrold, "Fulfillment of American Industrial Watch Manufacture: Royal Robbins Launches the Waltham Watch," 582.

[83] Moore, *Timing a Century: History of the Waltham Watch Company*, 26–27.

[84] Moore, *Timing a Century: History of the Waltham Watch Company*, 27.

[85] Eli Dennison, "1871, February 1. Sketch of Aaron's [Dennison] Life Written by His Brother Eli, to a Mr. Schilling.," in *Aaron Lufkin Dennison* (Columbia, PA: National Association of Watch & Clock Collectors, Inc., 2009), 109.

[86] Eliashab Tracy, "The American Watch Company (Letter Dated November 25, 1886)," *National Association of Watch and Clock Collectors' Bulletin*, no. 28 (April 1949): 274–75.

[87] Dennison, "1871, February 1. Sketch of Aaron's [Dennison] Life Written by His Brother Eli, to a Mr. Schilling.," 109.

[88] E.A. Marsh, *History (1921)*, ed. Richard Watkins, vol. RC-2, 2006, 12.

[89] Harrold, "Fulfillment of American Industrial Watch Manufacture: Royal Robbins Launches the Waltham Watch," 583–84.

[90] Watkins, *Watchmaking and the American System of Manufacturing (Revised)*, 36.

[91] Marsh, *History (1921)*, RC-2:12.

[92] Priestley, *Aaron Lufkin Dennison: An Industrial Pioneer and His Legacy*, 18.

[93] Marsh, *History (1921)*, RC-2:12.

[94] Marsh, RC-2:12.

[95] Robbins, "Treasurer's Report, 1870, American (Waltham) Watch Company," 5–6.

[96] Watkins, *Watchmaking and the American System of Manufacturing (Revised)*, 38.

[97] See David, *American and Swiss Watchmaking in 1876*, 75.

[98] See Abbott, *History of the American Waltham Watch Company of Waltham, Mass.*, 79.

[99] Harrold, "Fulfillment of American Industrial Watch Manufacture: Royal Robbins Launches the Waltham Watch," 581, 585–87.

[100] Harrold, "Fulfillment of American Industrial Watch Manufacture: Royal Robbins Launches the Waltham Watch," 587–88.

[101] Marsh, *History (1921)*, RC-2:12.

[102] Moore, *Timing a Century: History of the Waltham Watch Company*, 318.

[103] Marsh, *History (1921)*, RC-2:30.

[104] Harrold, "Fulfillment of American Industrial Watch Manufacture: Royal Robbins Launches the Waltham Watch," 587–91.

[105] Marsh, *History (1921)*, RC-2:15.

[106] Author's calculations based on Royal E. Robbins, "Treasurer's Report, 1859, American (Waltham) Watch Company," Annual Report to Shareholders (Waltham Watch Company, 1859), Vol. AD-1, Special Collections, Baker Library, Harvard Business School; See Watkins, *Watchmaking and the American System of Manufacturing (Revised)*, 24 for analysis of Dennison's efficiency metrics; Harrold, "Fulfillment of American Industrial Watch Manufacture: Royal Robbins Launches the Waltham Watch," 587–88.

[107] Harrold, "Fulfillment of American Industrial Watch Manufacture: Royal Robbins Launches the Waltham Watch," 587–88.

[108] Harrold, fig. 5.

[109] Technically, "models" (as I use the word) were referred to as grades, and variations within the grades were referred to as models. However, to avoid confusion to the non-technical reader, I use the word "model" and "grade" interchangeably in the colloquial sense to refer to the broader level of quality.

[110] Harrold, "Fulfillment of American Industrial Watch Manufacture: Royal Robbins Launches the Waltham Watch," 591–92.

[111] Harrold, fig. 5.

[112] Moore, *Timing a Century: History of the Waltham Watch Company*, 318. Also see Harrold, "Fulfillment of American Industrial Watch Manufacture: Royal Robbins Launches the Waltham Watch," 593.

[113] Robbins, "Treasurer's Report, 1859, American (Waltham) Watch Company."

[114] Robbins, 4.

[115] Robbins, "Treasurer's Report, 1862, American (Waltham) Watch Company," 4.

[116] Waltham was producing at a rate of about 12,000 a year in 1861 increasing to 19,000 by the spring of 1863. See Keith, "Treasurer's Report, 1861, American (Waltham) Watch Company," 1; Royal E. Robbins, "Treasurer's Report, 1863, American (Waltham) Watch Company," Annual Report to Shareholders (Waltham Watch Company, 1863), 1, Vol. AD-1, Special Collections, Baker Library, Harvard Business School.

[117] The wholesale price was $13 and the retail prices were generally at least double the wholesale cost. See Moore, *Timing a Century: History of the Waltham Watch Company*, 50.

[118] McCrossen, *Marking Modern Times*, 61.

[119] In addition to Geller's research, McCrossen concurs that soldiers would have spent 2 months wages for a reliable watch.

[120] "Watches: Beware of Counterfeits," *The Indiana State Sentinel*, April 14, 1862.

[121] "Watches: American Watches," *The Indiana State Sentinel*, April 29, 1863.

[122] Robbins, "Treasurer's Report, 1862, American (Waltham) Watch Company," 4.

[123] Moore, *Timing a Century: History of the Waltham Watch Company*, 50.

[124] Robbins, "Treasurer's Report, 1864, American (Waltham) Watch Company," 3.

[125] Robbins, "Treasurer's Report,1863, American (Waltham) Watch Company," 3.

[126] Author's calculations using the revenue and profit data reported by Waltham in its Annual Reports 1862 to 1866.

[127] Royal E. Robbins, "Treasurer's Report, 1860, American (Waltham) Watch Company," Annual Report to Shareholders (Waltham Watch Company, 1860), Vol. AD-1, Special Collections, Baker Library, Harvard Business School; Royal E. Robbins, "Treasurer's Report, 1865, American (Waltham) Watch Company," Annual Report to Shareholders (Waltham Watch Company, 1865), Vol. AD-1, Special Collections, Baker Library, Harvard Business School; Converted using Williamson, "Seven Ways to Compute the Relative Value of a U.S. Dollar Amount, 1774 to Present."

[128] Priestley, *Aaron Lufkin Dennison: An Industrial Pioneer and His Legacy*, 20; Converted using Williamson, "Seven Ways to Compute the Relative Value of a U.S. Dollar Amount, 1774 to Present."

[129] Robbins, "Treasurer's Report, 1865, American (Waltham) Watch Company," 5–6.

[130] E.C. Alft and William H. Briska, *Elgin Time: A History of the Elgin National Watch Company 1864-1968* (Elgin: Elgin Historical Society, 2003), 10–13.

[131] David, *American and Swiss Watchmaking in 1876*, 37.

[132] This database of Waltham patents is not peer reviewed, but is very exhaustive in its documenting Waltham's patents. The first patent on a

machine was in 1882, which is consistent with other sources and the author's discussions with experts. "Waltham Pocket Watch Patents | Pocket Watch Database."

133 Dan Clawson, *Bureaucracy and the Labor Process: The Transformation of U.S. Industry 1860-1920* (New York: Monthly Review Press, 2009), 80.

134 Author's calculations based on assembled data in "Waltham Pocket Watch Patents | Pocket Watch Database."

135 David, *American and Swiss Watchmaking in 1876*, 30.

136 Thank you to George Collord for discussions with the author on this topic. Additionally, thank you to Jon Weber, Tom McIntyre, and Bob Frishman for providing additional insight.

137 Alfred D. Chandler, *Scale and Scope: The Dynamics of Industrial Capitalism* (Cambridge, Mass.: Belknap Press, 2004), 228.

138 Wesley M. Cohen, Richard R. Nelson, and John P. Walsh, "Protecting Their Intellectual Assets: Appropriability Conditions and Why U.S. Manufacturing Firms Patent (or Not)," *National Bureau of Economic Research Working Papers Series*, no. Working Paper 7552 (February 2000): fig. 5, http://www.nber.org/papers/w7552.

139 Robbins, "Treasurer's Report, 1865, American (Waltham) Watch Company," 4–5.

140 Moore, *Timing a Century: History of the Waltham Watch Company*, sec. Appendix E.

141 Robbins, "Treasurer's Report, 1870, American (Waltham) Watch Company," 4.

142 Derived by the author from Charles W. Moore, "Papers of Charles W. Moore, 1845-1946" (Researcher's notes, 1945), Vol. ZA-1, Waltham Watch Company Records, Special Collections, Baker Library, Harvard Business School.

143 Moore, *Timing a Century: History of the Waltham Watch Company*, 73.

144 Alfred D. Chandler, *The Visible Hand: The Managerial Revolution in American Business* (Cambridge, Mass.: Belknap Press, 1977), 243–44.

145 Royal E. Robbins, "Treasurer's Report, 1867, American (Waltham) Watch Company," Annual Report to Shareholders (Waltham Watch Company, 1867), 6, Vol. AD-1, Special Collections, Baker Library, Harvard Business School.

146 Royal E. Robbins, "Treasurer's Report, 1877, American (Waltham) Watch Company," Annual Report to Shareholders (Waltham Watch Company, 1877), 5–6, Vol. AD-1, Special Collections, Baker Library, Harvard Business School.

147 Robbins, "Treasurer's Report, 1875, American (Waltham) Watch Company," 5.

148 Moore, *Timing a Century: History of the Waltham Watch Company*, 54.

149 "Sidelights of the Day: Show the Boss the Ad," *New York Times*, May 9, 1953, 253. The date or exact era of Ford's visit is unknown, but probably occurred in the 1890s.

150 Keith, *A Family Tale or History of American Watchmaking in Five Chapters (1883)*, 60–64.

151 James C. Watson, *American Watches: An Extract from the Report on Horology at the International Exhibition at Philadelphia, 1876* (New York: Robbins & Appleton, 1877), 28.

152 David, *American and Swiss Watchmaking in 1876*, 23.

153 Moore, "Papers of Charles W. Moore, 1845-1946." Average derived by the author. Based on Waltham's payroll records average wage from Oct to Dec 1876. This is likely biased high because the payroll includes some manager salaries; with estimated corrections, the average could be as low as $1.72.

154 Records show she usually made about $1.60 per day during the years 1874 and 1875. "Wage Rate Book, 1876, American (Waltham) Watch Company" (Waltham Watch Company Records, 1876), Vol. KB-1, Baker Library Special Collections, Harvard Business School. Wages converted using Williamson, "Seven Ways to Compute the Relative Value of a U.S. Dollar Amount, 1774 to Present."

155 See Michael C. Harrold, "The Industrial Process in American Watchmaking," *National Association of Watch and Clock Collectors' Bulletin*, December 1991, 634 which discusses the evolution from non-automated to fully automatic machinery at Waltham. Gitelman, "The Labor Force at Waltham Watch during the Civil War Era," 217 notes that Waltham had to train employees by 1866; Gitelman, 220 discusses the skill levels typically associated with various tasks. His research focuses on the Civil War when Waltham required skilled employees. By 1876, the machinery improved enough that Harrold indicates that semi-skilled was the norm.

156 Robbins, "Treasurer's Report, 1871, American (Waltham) Watch Company," 4–5.

157 Robbins, 4.

158 David, *American and Swiss Watchmaking in 1876*, 14.

159 David, 26.

160 Gitelman, "The Labor Force at Waltham Watch during the Civil War Era," 226.

161 Watson, *American Watches: An Extract from the Report on Horology at the International Exhibition at Philadelphia, 1876*, 7.

162 Swinton, "A Model Factory in a Model City: A Social Study of the Waltham Watch Factory," 10.

[163] Swinton, 10; David, *American and Swiss Watchmaking in 1876*, 24; See Stark, "Companies Have Been Setting Equal Pay Policies (and Failing at Them) for More than 100 Years" for a further analysis.

[164] Swinton, "A Model Factory in a Model City: A Social Study of the Waltham Watch Factory," 7.

[165] "Wage Rate Book, 1876, American (Waltham) Watch Company." Derived by the author.

[166] David, *American and Swiss Watchmaking in 1876*, 24.

[167] "The Watch as a Growth Industry," 36.

[168] David, *American and Swiss Watchmaking in 1876*, 25.

[169] See "Wage Rate Book, 1876, American (Waltham) Watch Company" for composition of departments; David, *American and Swiss Watchmaking in 1876*, 25.

[170] Robbins, "Treasurer's Report, 1875, American (Waltham) Watch Company," 7.

[171] David, *American and Swiss Watchmaking in 1876*, 21.

[172] Peter N. Stearns, *The Industrial Revolution in World History*, 3rd ed. (Cambridge, Mass.: Westview Press, 2007), 71.

[173] Bally and Dubied, *Industry and Manufactures in the United States: Look Out for Yourselves!*, 25.

[174] Swinton, "A Model Factory in a Model City: A Social Study of the Waltham Watch Factory," 14.

[175] Gitelman, *Workingmen of Waltham*, 154.

[176] Gitelman, 73.

[177] Swinton, "A Model Factory in a Model City: A Social Study of the Waltham Watch Factory," 16.

[178] Swinton, 16.

[179] Marsh, *History of Early Watchmaking in America, 1890*, RC-1:9.

[180] Marsh, RC-1:9.

[181] Gitelman, "The Labor Force at Waltham Watch during the Civil War Era," 220–21.

[182] Marsh, RC-1:9.

[183] David, 26.

[184] David, 23.

[185] David, 27 David noted that both Waltham and Elgin had very clear, written regulations that governed and incentivized employee innovation and improvements.

[186] Leonard Waldo, "The Mechanical Art of Watchmaking," *Van Nostrand's Engineering Magazine*, July 1, 1886, 50.

[187] Edward Bally would describe this phenomenon writing that the "European works as he has learned to do, that the master continually teaches his apprentice the same routine, while the American seeks unceasingly to simplify the manipulation, to invent and to apply every possible improvement." Bally and Dubied, *Industry and Manufactures in the United States: Look Out for Yourselves!*, 5–6.

[188] David, *American and Swiss Watchmaking in 1876*, 8.

[189] David, *American and Swiss Watchmaking in 1876*, 21.

[190] David, 21.

[191] David, 25.

[192] Frank T. Reuter, "John Swinton's Paper," *Journal of Labor History* 1, no. 3 (1960): 301.

[193] Reuter, 301.

[194] Reuter, 299.

[195] Swinton, "A Model Factory in a Model City: A Social Study of the Waltham Watch Factory," 8.

[196] Gitelman, "The Labor Force at Waltham Watch during the Civil War Era," 230.

[197] Gitelman, *Workingmen of Waltham*, 74.

[198] Moore, *Timing a Century: History of the Waltham Watch Company*, 65.

[199] Landes, "Watchmaking: A Case Study in Enterprise and Change," 16.

[200] Samuel H.M. Byers, *Switzerland and the Swiss, by an American Resident* (Zurich: Zurich, Orell, Fussli & Co, 1875), 75.

[201] Richard Watkins, ed., "Manufacture of Watches in Switzerland, 1842" (The Saturday Evening Magazine, October 1842), 2.

[202] Edward Young, "Labor in Europe and America," Government (Washington, D.C.: United States Government Printing Office, 1876), 606.

[203] Byers, *Switzerland and the Swiss, by an American Resident*, 77–78.

[204] Eugene Jaquet and Alfred Chapuis, *Technique and History of the Swiss Watch* (New York: Spring Books, 1970), 48–49. Much of the legend of Richard seems to be exactly that – legend.

[205] Landes, *Revolution in Time*, 259.

[206] Amy Glasmeier, *Manufacturing Time: Global Competition in the Watch Industry, 1795-2000*, Perspectives on Economic Change (New York: Guilford Press, 2000), 97.

[207] Laurence Marti, *A Region in Time: A Socio-Economic History of the Swiss Valley of St. Imier and the Surrounding Area, 1700-2007*, trans. Rosamund Bandi-Tebbut (St. Imier: Editions des Longines, 2007), 58.

[208] Marti, 60.

[209] Young, "Labor in Europe and America," 623.

[210] Landes, *Revolution in Time*, 242.

[211] Landes, 238.

[212] Pierre-Yves Donzé, *History of the Swiss Watch Industry: From Jacques David to Nicolas Hayek*, trans. Richard Watkins (Bern, Switzerland: Peter Lang, 2015), 6–7. Donzé suggests that watchmaking spread "from an endogenous development process. This region enjoyed its own commercial networks, organized on a global scale by some of the trading families of the city of Neuchatel…and these offered ways to sell watches." In other words, entrepreneurs figure out ways to make money from what works – watches worked.

[213] Van den Steen and Stark, "Stealing Time: America's Disruption of the Swiss Watch Industry (718-500)," 2–3.

[214] Marti, *A Region in Time: A Socio-Economic History of the Swiss Valley of St. Imier and the Surrounding Area, 1700-2007*, 62.

[215] Moore, *Timing a Century: History of the Waltham Watch Company*, 232 notes that it took about 7.5 days for a single Swiss watch. Also see Van den Steen and Stark, "Stealing Time: America's Disruption of the Swiss Watch Industry (718-500)," 3.

[216] Byers, *Switzerland and the Swiss, by an American Resident*, 8.

[217] David Wells, "Swiss Watchmaking and Musical Boxes: A History of Mechanical Industry in Geneva and the Jura Mountains," *National Association of Watch and Clock Collectors' Bulletin*, no. 38.304 (1996): 622.

[218] Landes, *Revolution in Time*, 261–62.

[219] Pierre-Yves Donzé, *Longines, from a Family Business to a Global Brand*, trans. Rosamund Bandi-Tebbut (St. Imier: Editions des Longines, 2012), 35.

[220] "The Watch as a Growth Industry," 31.

[221] Walker, "International Exhibition 1876 Reports and Awards Group XXI," 118.

[222] Donzé, *Longines, from a Family Business to a Global Brand*, 34.

[223] Donzé, 44–45.

[224] "The Watch as a Growth Industry," 32.

[225] "Waltham Watches (Advertisement)," *Cleveland Morning Herald*, July 15, 1871, sec. Classified Ads.

[226] Watson, *American Watches: An Extract from the Report on Horology at the International Exhibition at Philadelphia, 1876*, 7.

[227] Waldo, "The Mechanical Art of Watchmaking," 50. There is no indication as to when Waltham began this scientific approach to metal testing, but it is presumed to have been in use in some form prior to the Centennial Exhibition.

[228] Watson, *American Watches: An Extract from the Report on Horology at the International Exhibition at Philadelphia, 1876*, 12–13.

[229] Watson, *American Watches: An Extract from the Report on Horology at the International Exhibition at Philadelphia, 1876*, 12–13.

[230] Watson, 13.

[231] Robbins, "Treasurer's Report, 1876, American (Waltham) Watch Company," 1, 9.

[232] Chandler, *The Visible Hand*, 281–82.

[233] Robbins, "Treasurer's Report, 1879, American (Waltham) Watch Company," 1.

[234] Robbins, "Treasurer's Report, 1876, American (Waltham) Watch Company," 8.

[235] See Robbins, 8.

[236] "Ledger B, American Watch Co, 1864-1876" (Ledger, 1876), 130–31, Vol. C-1, Waltham Watch Company Records, Special Collections, Baker Library, Harvard Business School.

[237] Leslie Nesky, ed., "Waltham Free Press, 04 February 1876 in 'The American Watch Company 1876,'" *National Association of Watch and Clock Collectors' Bulletin*, The American Watch Company 1876, April 2004, 161.

[238] Robbins, "Treasurer's Report, 1876, American (Waltham) Watch Company," 8.

[239] While Robbins and other sources cite 16 machines as the number that will appear, article accounts from the Exhibition cite 20 machines. *Waltham Free Press*, 7 July 1876, published in "The American Watch Company 1876", compiled Leslie Nesky in the *National Association of Watch and Clock Collectors Bulletin*, April, 2004, p. 166. Additionally, the Centennial judges recorded the following types of machines on display: "Screw-making machines, screw-polishing machines, wheel-cutting engine, damaskeening machine, pinion-cutting machine, pinion-polishing machine, pinion-leaf-polishing machine, staking-tools, opening wheel machine, colleting-wheel machine, jewel-turning lathe, jewel drilling lathe, etc." See Walker, "International Exhibition 1876 Reports and Awards Group XXI," 52.

[240] Robbins, "Treasurer's Report, 1876, American (Waltham) Watch Company," 7.

[241] Bruno Giberti, *Designing the Centennial: A History of the 1876 International Exhibition in Philadelphia*, Material Worlds (Lexington: The University of Kentucky Press, 2002), 102.

[242] Edouard Favre-Perret, "Philadelphia Exhibition 1876: Presented to the Federal High Council on the Horology Industry," trans. Richard Watkins (Winterthur: Federal High Council on the Horology Industry, 2004 1877), 3, Richard Watkins, Tasmania.

[243] Leslie Nesky, ed., "Waltham Free Press, 05 May 1876 in 'The American Watch Company 1876,'" *National Association of Watch and Clock Collectors' Bulletin*, The American Watch Company 1876, April 2004, 163.

244 McCabe, *The Illustrated History of the Centennial Exhibition*, 333.

245 Leslie Nesky, ed., "Waltham Sentinel, 26 May 1876 in 'The American Watch Company 1876,'" *National Association of Watch and Clock Collectors' Bulletin*, The American Watch Company 1876, April 2004, 163.

246 Favre-Perret refers to all American watch producers, but in the following few sentences, demonstrates the most alarm with Waltham. Favre-Perret, "Philadelphia Exhibition 1876: Presented to the Federal High Council on the Horology Industry," 3.

247 Favre-Perret, 4.

248 There are no riveting accounts of Elgin's tool display as can be found with Waltham. In fact, the main references to Elgin are to its watch display case. Were it not for the Centennial Catalog documenting its presence, Elgin's tool display goes largely overlooked. See *Official Catalogue of the International Exhibition of 1876 (Part 1)*, 2nd ed. (Philadelphia: Centennial Catalogue Company, 1876), 136.

249 Edward Guyer, "Letter to the U.S. Centennial Commission (September 11, 1875)," September 11, 1875, Vol 230.26, Box A-1526, Centennial Exhibition Collection, City of Philadelphia Archives.

250 "Letter to the U.S. Centennial Commission (November 18, 1875)," November 18, 1875, Vol 230.26, Box A-1526, Centennial Exhibition Collection, City of Philadelphia Archives; Guyer, "Letter to the U.S. Centennial Commission (September 11, 1875)."

251 Guyer, "Letter to the U.S. Centennial Commission (September 11, 1875)."

252 McCabe, *The Illustrated History of the Centennial Exhibition*, 403.

253 McCabe, 402.

254 Favre-Perret, "Philadelphia Exhibition 1876: Presented to the Federal High Council on the Horology Industry," 6.

255 McCabe, *The Illustrated History of the Centennial Exhibition*, 402.

256 Favre-Perret, "Philadelphia Exhibition 1876: Presented to the Federal High Council on the Horology Industry," 8.

257 O'Malley, *Keeping Watch: A History of American Time*, 152–55.

258 Giberti, *Designing the Centennial: A History of the 1876 International Exhibition in Philadelphia*, 35.

259 Favre-Perret, "Watchmaking in America: A Foreigner's Testimony," 34.

260 James C. Watson, "Circular by James C. Watson, February 25, 1879" (The Bell Telephone Company), Library of Congress, accessed February 23, 2018, https://www.loc.gov/item/magbell.28500125/.

261 Jaquet and Chapuis, *Technique and History of the Swiss Watch*, 179.

262 Watson, *American Watches: An Extract from the Report on Horology at the International Exhibition at Philadelphia, 1876*, 26.

263 Watson, *American Watches: An Extract from the Report on Horology at the International Exhibition at Philadelphia, 1876*, 14.

264 David, *American and Swiss Watchmaking in 1876*, 6.

265 Watson, *American Watches: An Extract from the Report on Horology at the International Exhibition at Philadelphia, 1876*, 27.

266 Watson, 15–16.

267 "Award Citation for the American Watch Company, Report of Awards Group XXII" (Centennial Commission, September 1876), Vol 230, Box A-1514, Centennial Exhibition Collection, City of Philadelphia Archives.

268 "Award Citation for the American Watch Company, Report of Awards Group XXII."

269 Walker, "International Exhibition 1876 Reports and Awards Group XXI," 52.

270 McCabe, *The Illustrated History of the Centennial Exhibition*, 195.

271 "Wage Rate Book, 1876, American (Waltham) Watch Company."

272 "Ambrose Webster Biography," *The Keystone Magazine*, December 1892, 1171.

273 See McCabe, *The Illustrated History of the Centennial Exhibition*, sec. Awards.

274 "Ambrose Webster Biography," 1171.

275 Moore, *Timing a Century: History of the Waltham Watch Company*, 224–25.

276 David, "Letter from Jacques David to Ernest Francillon, September 1876."

277 *Proceedings at the Celebration of the Sesqui-Centennial of the Town of Waltham, Held in Music Hall, on Monday, January 16th, 1888* (Waltham, Mass.: E.L. Berry, 1893), 57.

278 Tom Nicholas and Matthew Guilford, "Samuel Slater & Francis Cabot Lowell: The Factory System in U.S. Cotton Manufacturing (9-814-065)," Case Study (Boston: Harvard Business School Publishing, 2016), 3.

279 J. R. (John Raymond) Harris, *Industrial Espionage and Technology Transfer: Britain and France in the Eighteenth Century* (England: Ashgate Pub, 1998), 362.

280 Richard S. Friedman, "War By Other Means: Economic Intelligence and Industrial Espionage [Review Essay]," *Parameters* 3, no. 28 (Autumn 1998): 154.

281 Chaim M. Rosenberg, *The Life and Times of Francis Cabot Lowell, 1775-1817* (New York: Lexington Books, 2010), 203–14.

282 See Paul Brians, "Emulate / Imitate," *Common Errors in English Usage and More: Washington State University* (blog), May 24, 2016, https://brians.wsu.edu/2016/05/25/emulate-imitate/ which succinctly explains this common nuance.

[283] The author thanks Dr. Alexis McCrossen for her observation of the importance of imitation versus emulation in this story.

[284] Rosenberg, *The Life and Times of Francis Cabot Lowell, 1775-1817*, 203–14.

[285] Jacques David, *Rapport à la Société intercantonale des industries du Jura sur la fabrication de l'horlogerie aux Etats-Unis, 1876* (St. Imier: la Compagnie des montres Longines Francillon, 1992), chap. Preface.

[286] Jacques David, "Letter from Jacques David to Ernest Francillon, September 1876," in *Longines, from a Family Business to a Global Brand*, by Pierre-Yves Donzé, trans. Rosamund Bandi-Tebbut (St. Imeir: Editions des Longines, 2012), 48.

[287] David, 48.

[288] David, *American and Swiss Watchmaking in 1876*, 27.

[289] David did not document his trip's exact route. Crescent Street is the probable route taken as the factory sits on Crescent St and the river. I have taken David's descriptions of what he saw inside the factory and extrapolated the sights and sounds that David would have seen and heard based on other contemporary accounts. I have specified what events are probable versus those that he specifically mentioned.

[290] David, *American and Swiss Watchmaking in 1876*, 20.

[291] David never specified what type of disguise he used to gather information, whether that of a worker or a distinguished visitor. The most probable infiltration (short of a break-in, which he does not mention) was entering as a common worker.

[292] David, *American and Swiss Watchmaking in 1876*, 20.

[293] Stearns, *The Industrial Revolution in World History*, 70.

[294] One study found that French Canadians were almost 7% of the Massachusetts population by 1891. See William MacDonald, "The French Canadians in New England," *The Quarterly Journal of Economics* 12, no. 3 (1898): 251.

[295] See chapter 18 and 19 for Waltham's methods of production noted by David. David, *American and Swiss Watchmaking in 1876*, 22.

[296] David, 20.

[297] David, 20.

[298] David, *American and Swiss Watchmaking in 1876*, 20. Also, see chapters 14, 15, 16 for further analysis of Swiss working conditions.

[299] David, 24.

[300] Swinton, "A Model Factory in a Model City: A Social Study of the Waltham Watch Factory," 6.

[301] David, "Letter from Jacques David to Ernest Francillon, September 1876," 48.

[302] David, *American and Swiss Watchmaking in 1876*, 25.

[303] David, 25.

[304] David, "Letter from Jacques David to Ernest Francillon, September 1876," 48.

[305] David, 48.

[306] David, *American and Swiss Watchmaking in 1876*, 9.

[307] Establishing the earliest uses of the term 'Industrial Espionage' is by no means a conclusive process. In historical record databases, the term begins around WWI and slowly gained prominence. Peter Heims claims the term came into common usage around the 1960s. See Peter Heims, *Countering Industrial Espionage* (England: 20th Century Security Education, 1982), 5.

[308] Susan Brenner and Anthony Crescenzi, "State Sponsored Crime: The Futility of the Economics Espionage Act," *Houston Journal of International Law* 28, no. 2 (2006): 394–97.

[309] Omid Nodoushani and Patricia Nodoushani, "Industrial Espionage: The Dark Side of the Digital Age," *Competitiveness Review* 12, no. 2 (2002): 97.

[310] Francillon, *History of Longines*, 33.

[311] Francillon, 33.

[312] Francillon, 33.

[313] Francillon, 33.

[314] David, "Letter from Jacques David to Ernest Francillon, September 1876," 48.

[315] Andrew Crane, "In the Company of Spies: When Competitive Intelligence Gathering Becomes Industrial Espionage," *Business Horizons*, 2005, 234.

[316] Heims, *Countering Industrial Espionage*, 12.

[317] Brenner and Crescenzi, "State Sponsored Crime: The Futility of the Economics Espionage Act," 396.

[318] Heims, *Countering Industrial Espionage*, 74–75.

[319] Heims, 80.

[320] The first known reference to David as an industrial spy was written in the *Swiss Journal of History* (1987) where David was briefly referred to as "En veritable espion industriel" which translates to "a real industrial spy." Barrelet, "Les Résistances à l'innovation Dans l'industrie Horlogère Des Montagnes Neuchâteloises à La Fin Du XIXe Siècle," 398. The paragraph that references David as a spy has been repeated and modified on other websites since, including on David's French Wikipedia entry. The same descriptor is used in a recent informational pamphlet highlighting the watchmaking heroes of St. Imier, David's hometown. Also see "Jacques David and the Shock of Philadelphia" (Energies Horlogeres), accessed July 18, 2018, http://energies-horlogeres.m-ici.ch/lieux/2.

[321] Swinton, "A Model Factory in a Model City: A Social Study of the Waltham Watch Factory," 6.

[322] Robbins, "Treasurer's Report, 1876, American (Waltham) Watch Company," 8.

[323] David, "Letter from Jacques David to Ernest Francillon, September 1876," 48.

[324] Royal E. Robbins, "Treasurer's Report, 1869, American (Waltham) Watch Company," Annual Report to Shareholders (Waltham Watch Company, 1869), 3, Vol. AD-1, Special Collections, Baker Library, Harvard Business School.

[325] Henry Ganney, "A Lecture Upon the American Watch Manufacture, Jan 14, 1869," in *Lancashire Watch Company: History and Watches*, by John G. Platt (Edinburgh: Inbeat Publications, 2016), 28.

[326] Robbins, "Treasurer's Report, 1869, American (Waltham) Watch Company," 3.

[327] Phillip C. Wright and Geraldine Roy, "Industrial Espionage and Competitive Intelligence: One You Do; One You Do Not," *Journal of Workplace Learning* 11.2 (1999): 53–59.

[328] Wright and Roy, "Industrial Espionage and Competitive Intelligence: One You Do; One You Do Not," 53–59.

[329] Heims, *Countering Industrial Espionage*, 81–82.

[330] Heims, 81–82.

[331] David, *American and Swiss Watchmaking in 1876*, 9.

[332] David, n. 11. Watkins estimates that none of David's sources were ever revealed. However, David was careless in his personal correspondence and identified Ambrose Webster in a personal letter.

[333] David, *American and Swiss Watchmaking in 1876*, 9.

[334] David, *American and Swiss Watchmaking in 1876*, 48.

[335] David, 78.

[336] David, 81.

[337] Moore, *Timing a Century: History of the Waltham Watch Company*, 51.

[338] David, *American and Swiss Watchmaking in 1876*, 9.

[339] David was able to get Waltham's dividend schedule. These were probably somewhat public.

[340] See "Ledger B, American Watch Co, 1864-1876," 130–31.

[341] David, *American and Swiss Watchmaking in 1876*, 15.

[342] David, *American and Swiss Watchmaking in 1876*, 23.

[343] This is figured by taking the estimated number of workers reported and their average wages and producing a weighted average i.e. 365 x $2.50 + 310 x $1.00 +…

[344] On John Swinton's visit to the factory in 1887, he reported "The account books of the watch factory, indicating the pay of all hands for each and every week of the year, were placed at my service." However, David's experience does not indicate that he had access to the ledgers. As a labor reformer of the era, it would be perfectly plausible that Robbins would open his books for Swinton to prove that Waltham was complying with reforms and thus stay out of the press. See Swinton, p. 10.

[345] Waltham's actual averages are skewed higher as they include wages for foremen who were higher paid and which David catalogued separately. Therefore, David was almost exact in his estimates.

[346] Based on Moore, "Papers of Charles W. Moore, 1845-1946." by taking the monthly wage and dividing by the number of employees paid, divided by 27 days per month.

[347] Nesky, "Waltham Free Press, 16 June 1876 in 'The American Watch Company 1876,'" 166.

[348] *Official Catalogue of the International Exhibition of 1876 (Part 1)*, 69.

[349] David, *American and Swiss Watchmaking in 1876*, 74.

[350] David, "Letter from Jacques David to Ernest Francillon, September 1876."

[351] Leslie Nesky, ed., "Waltham Free Press, 24 Nov 1876 in 'The American Watch Company 1876,'" *National Association of Watch and Clock Collectors' Bulletin*, The American Watch Company 1876, April 2004, 171.

[352] Leslie Nesky, ed., "Waltham Sentinel, 14 Jul 1876 in 'The American Watch Company 1876,'" *National Association of Watch and Clock Collectors' Bulletin*, The American Watch Company 1876, April 2004, 167.

[353] David, "Letter from Jacques David to Ernest Francillon, September 1876."

[354] David, "Letter from Jacques David to Ernest Francillon, September 1876."

[355] "Ambrose Webster Biography," 1171.

[356] Bally and Dubied, *Industry and Manufactures in the United States: Look Out for Yourselves!*, sec. Translator's Note (viii).

[357] McCabe, *The Illustrated History of the Centennial Exhibition*, 854.

[358] Bally and Dubied, *Industry and Manufactures in the United States: Look Out for Yourselves!*, 11.

[359] McCabe, *The Illustrated History of the Centennial Exhibition*, 854.

[360] Watson, *American Watches: An Extract from the Report on Horology at the International Exhibition at Philadelphia, 1876*, 32, 34.

[361] Favre-Perret, "Philadelphia Exhibition 1876: Presented to the Federal High Council on the Horology Industry," 3–4.

[362] Favre-Perret, 3–4.

[363] David, *American and Swiss Watchmaking in 1876*, 70.

[364] Robbins, "Treasurer's Report, 1877, American (Waltham) Watch Company," 7.

365 Favre-Perret, "Watchmaking in America: A Foreigner's Testimony," 36.

366 "American Watches," *The Inter Ocean,* December 22, 1876, 4.

367 "American Manufactures," *The McHenry Plaindealer,* September 5, 1877, 3.

368 "American Watches," 4.

369 "Timekeepers," *The North American,* February 7, 1877.

370 Robbins, "Treasurer's Report, 1877, American (Waltham) Watch Company," 5–6.

371 "Watchmaking by Machinery," 92.

372 "Watchmaking by Machinery," 92.

373 "Watchmaking by Machinery," 93.

374 David, *American and Swiss Watchmaking in 1876,* 72.

375 David's first report is dated January 22, 1877. See David, *Rapport à la Société intercantonale des industries du Jura sur la fabrication de l'horlogerie aux Etats-Unis, 1876.*

376 Favre-Perret, "Watchmaking in America: A Foreigner's Testimony," 35.

377 David, *American and Swiss Watchmaking in 1876,* 8.

378 David, 12.

379 David, 38.

380 Favre-Perret, "Philadelphia Exhibition 1876: Presented to the Federal High Council on the Horology Industry," 11.

381 David, *American and Swiss Watchmaking in 1876,* 82.

382 David, 72.

383 Francillon, *History of Longines,* 32.

384 David, *American and Swiss Watchmaking in 1876,* 72.

385 Glasmeier, *Manufacturing Time,* 97.

386 Jean-Marc Olivier, "Industrial Landscapes in the Jura Mountains during the 19th Century: So Many Invisible Hands" (2009), 3–4.

387 J.S. Nicholson, "The Effects of Machinery on Wages, 1877" (Cambridge, Deighton, Bell, and Co., 1878), 13.

388 David, *American and Swiss Watchmaking in 1876,* 82.

389 David, 37.

390 David, *American and Swiss Watchmaking in 1876,* 73–75.

391 David, 73.

392 David, 73.

393 David, 73.

394 In his landmark book *Time Telling Through the Ages,* Harry Brearley describes the Swiss system: "Most establishments specialize in the manufacture of particular parts and these parts are then assembled in other factories. Some fifty different trades there are working separately to

produce the parts. And the manufacturer, whose work is chiefly that of finishing and assembling, takes a large profit for inspection and for the prestige of his name." Harry C. Brearley, *Timetelling Through the Ages* (Doubleday, Page & Co. for Robert H. Ingersol & Bros., 1919), 182, https://catalog.hathitrust.org/Record/001045370.

[395] David, *American and Swiss Watchmaking in 1876*, 73.

[396] David, 73.

[397] Glasmeier, *Manufacturing Time*, 139–43.

[398] Landes, *Revolution in Time*, 324.

[399] DeLong, "Memories of America's Noted Horologist: Theophilus Gribi," 34.

[400] See "A Practical Treastise on Adjusting [Review]," *Jeweler's Circular & Horological Review* 27 (November 1, 1893): 22; Orville R. Hagans, "American Watchmakers' Institute's Heritage," *Horological Times*, May 1978, 12–13.

[401] DeLong, "Memories of America's Noted Horologist: Theophilus Gribi," 34.

[402] David Christianson, "Watch Repair in America: Part 1," *Horological Times*, December 2007, 10.

[403] Lange was a German producer based in Dresden but was a prominent figure that participated in the dialogue following the Centennial Exhibition and specifically debated with David about his report. See page 77 (David).

[404] David, *American and Swiss Watchmaking in 1876*, 77.

[405] David, 76.

[406] Favre-Perret, "Philadelphia Exhibition 1876: Presented to the Federal High Council on the Horology Industry," 12.

[407] Glasmeier, *Manufacturing Time*, 136.

[408] See Glasmeier, *Manufacturing Time*, 136; Donzé, *History of the Swiss Watch Industry*, 29.

[409] "Swiss Watches for the American Market," *The Jewelers' Circular and Horological Review*, January 1885, 400.

[410] Richard N. Langlois, "Schumpeter and Personal Capitalism Economics Working Paper" (University of Connecticut, March 1996), 18.

[411] Donzé, *History of the Swiss Watch Industry*, 40.

[412] David, *American and Swiss Watchmaking in 1876*, sec. Translators' preface.

[413] David, 9.

[414] David, 9; Jean-Marc Barrelet and Jacqueline Henry Bédat, *Preface to the Rapport à la Société intercantonale des industries du Jura sur la fabrication de l'horlogerie aux Etats-Unis, 1876 [Translation of Preface unpublished]*, trans. Richard Watkins, Longines (St. Imeir: Longines, 1992).

[415] See Barrelet, "Les Résistances à l'innovation Dans l'industrie Horlogère Des Montagnes Neuchâteloises à La Fin Du XIXe Siècle."

[416] See David, *Rapport à la Société intercantonale des industries du Jura sur la fabrication de l'horlogerie aux Etats-Unis, 1876.*

[417] Donzé, *History of the Swiss Watch Industry*, 34.

[418] David, *American and Swiss Watchmaking in 1876*, 72.

[419] *Handbook for Switzerland and the Adjacent Regions of the Alps*, 19th ed. (London: Edward Stanford, 1905), 72.

[420] Marti, *A Region in Time: A Socio-Economic History of the Swiss Valley of St. Imier and the Surrounding Area, 1700-2007*, 106–11.

[421] Favre-Perret, "Philadelphia Exhibition 1876: Presented to the Federal High Council on the Horology Industry," sec. Translator's introduction.

[422] Favre-Perret, 10–11.

[423] Donzé, *History of the Swiss Watch Industry*, 35–36.

[424] Frank Webb, *Switzerland of the Swiss* (New York: Scribner, 1913), 66.

[425] Donzé, *History of the Swiss Watch Industry*, 35–36.

[426] Olivier, "Industrial Landscapes in the Jura Mountains during the 19th Century: So Many Invisible Hands," 3.

[427] Marti, *A Region in Time: A Socio-Economic History of the Swiss Valley of St. Imier and the Surrounding Area, 1700-2007*, 123.

[428] Olivier, "Industrial Landscapes in the Jura Mountains during the 19th Century: So Many Invisible Hands," 1–2.

[429] Francillon, *History of Longines*, 35.

[430] "Character of the Swiss Watchmaker," *The Jewelers' Circular and Horological Review*, January 9, 1895, 42.

[431] Marti, *A Region in Time: A Socio-Economic History of the Swiss Valley of St. Imier and the Surrounding Area, 1700-2007*, 119.

[432] Boules is a game similar to bocce or lawn bowling.

[433] Marti, *A Region in Time: A Socio-Economic History of the Swiss Valley of St. Imier and the Surrounding Area, 1700-2007*, 119.

[434] David, *American and Swiss Watchmaking in 1876*, 20.

[435] Bally and Dubied, 24–25.

[436] Donzé, *History of the Swiss Watch Industry*, 55.

[437] *Handbook for Switzerland and the Adjacent Regions of the Alps*, 72.

[438] Landes, *Revolution in Time*, 323.

[439] Donzé, *History of the Swiss Watch Industry*, 34–35.

[440] Pierre-Yves Donzé, "Culture technique et enseignement professionnel dans les écoles d'horlogerie suisses (1850-1920)," *Histoire de l'éducation*, no.

119 (July 1, 2008): paras. 7–8, https://doi.org/10.4000/histoire-education.1841.

441 Marti, *A Region in Time: A Socio-Economic History of the Swiss Valley of St. Imier and the Surrounding Area, 1700-2007*, 151.

442 Walker, "International Exhibition 1876 Reports and Awards Group XXI," 118.

443 David, *American and Swiss Watchmaking in 1876*, 75.

444 Donzé, "Culture technique et enseignement professionnel dans les écoles d'horlogerie suisses (1850-1920)."

445 David, *American and Swiss Watchmaking in 1876*, 75.

446 Donzé, "Culture technique et enseignement professionnel dans les écoles d'horlogerie suisses (1850-1920)," para. 14.

447 Donzé, para. 14.

448 Donzé, paras. 32–33.

449 Pierre-Yves Donzé, "The Creation of Schools of Watchmaking," *Horlogerie Suisse*, October 11, 2007, Online edition, Accessed via web archive (dated 03/03/2016), http://www.horlogerie-suisse.com/articles/watcharound/La-creation-des-ecoles-d-horlogerie-m11707.html.

450 Marti, *A Region in Time: A Socio-Economic History of the Swiss Valley of St. Imier and the Surrounding Area, 1700-2007*, 151.

451 Bally and Dubied, *Industry and Manufactures in the United States: Look Out for Yourselves!*, 36.

452 Thank you to Diana Volonakis for her correspondence and discussion with the author about David's enduring role in the education system in Switzerland.

453 Marti, *A Region in Time: A Socio-Economic History of the Swiss Valley of St. Imier and the Surrounding Area, 1700-2007*, 152.

454 Marti, 153.

455 Marti, *A Region in Time: A Socio-Economic History of the Swiss Valley of St. Imier and the Surrounding Area, 1700-2007*, 109.

456 Marti, 110–11.

457 "History of Longines," accessed February 24, 2019, https://www.longines.com/company/history/19th/1876.

458 David, *American and Swiss Watchmaking in 1876*, 29.

459 David, 19.

460 David, 72.

461 Favre-Perret, "Watchmaking in America: A Foreigner's Testimony," 35.

462 Favre-Perret, "Philadelphia Exhibition 1876: Presented to the Federal High Council on the Horology Industry," 11.

[463] Favre-Perret, 11.

[464] David, *American and Swiss Watchmaking in 1876*, 75.

[465] Marti, *A Region in Time: A Socio-Economic History of the Swiss Valley of St. Imier and the Surrounding Area, 1700-2007*, 152–53 notes many other prominent watchmakers calling for the same action, including Chopard, Ducommon, among others.

[466] Walker, "International Exhibition 1876 Reports and Awards Group XXI," 117.

[467] Marti, *A Region in Time: A Socio-Economic History of the Swiss Valley of St. Imier and the Surrounding Area, 1700-2007*, 152–57.

[468] Marti, *A Region in Time: A Socio-Economic History of the Swiss Valley of St. Imier and the Surrounding Area, 1700-2007*, 152–57.

[469] Webb, *Switzerland of the Swiss*, 62.

[470] David, *American and Swiss Watchmaking in 1876*, 74–75.

[471] David, *American and Swiss Watchmaking in 1876*, 74–75.

[472] "Survey: World Willing to Pay More for Swissness," The Local CH, July 15, 2016, https://www.thelocal.ch/20160715/survey-world-willing-to-pay-more-for-swissness.

[473] *The Inter-Ocean [Chicago]*, December 22, 1876, 4.

[474] James G. Blaine, "The Man of Maine [Speech]," *St. Louis Globe Democrat*, September 24, 1880.

[475] Douglas A. Irwin, "Tariffs and Growth in Late Nineteenth Century America," *Department of Economics, Dartmouth College*, June 2000, 2–5.

[476] "Watch-Making," *Milwaukee Daily Journal*, October 4, 1884.

[477] Robbins, "Treasurer's Report, 1878, American (Waltham) Watch Company," 7.

[478] Robbins, "Treasurer's Report, 1877, American (Waltham) Watch Company," 5.

[479] Robbins, "Treasurer's Report, 1878, American (Waltham) Watch Company," 7.

[480] "Sales B, 1877-1884" (Sales Journal, 1884), Vol. O-4, Waltham Watch Company Records, Special Collections, Baker Library, Harvard Business School.

[481] Robbins, "Treasurer's Report, 1878, American (Waltham) Watch Company," 6.

[482] Robbins, 6.

[483] "United States Centennial Commission," *Reading Times*, August 14, 1877, 4.

[484] "American 'Waltham' Watch Agency," *The New Orleans Daily Democrat*, April 6, 1877, 4.

[485] "Watchmaking by Machinery," 93.

[486] "Watchmaking by Machinery," 94.

[487] Robbins, "Treasurer's Report, 1878, American (Waltham) Watch Company."

[488] Glasmeier, *Manufacturing Time*, 119.

[489] Moore, *Timing a Century: History of the Waltham Watch Company*, 83.

[490] Robbins, "Treasurer's Report, 1879, American (Waltham) Watch Company," 4-5.

[491] Robbins, "Treasurer's Report, 1876, American (Waltham) Watch Company."

[492] Robbins, "Treasurer's Report, 1877, American (Waltham) Watch Company."

[493] Royal E. Robbins, "Treasurer's Report, 1883, American (Waltham) Watch Company," Annual Report to Shareholders (Waltham Watch Company, 1883), Vol. AD-2, Special Collections, Baker Library, Harvard Business School In this report, Robbins gave the results from 1882. Generally in this book, I have reported results in the year Robbins wrote about them, but in this specific case, I have reported the results based on the year they would have actually occurred.

[494] "The Philadelphia Exhibition of 1876…," *Boston Daily Advertiser*, February 20, 1884, Iss. 44 edition.

[495] "Swiss Watches for the American Market."

[496] Royal E. Robbins, "Treasurer's Report, 1886, American (Waltham) Watch Company," Annual Report to Shareholders (Waltham Watch Company, 1886), 6, Vol. AD-2, Special Collections, Baker Library, Harvard Business School.

[497] Royal E. Robbins, "Treasurer's Report, 1888, American (Waltham) Watch Company," Annual Report to Shareholders (Waltham Watch Company, 1888), Vol. AD-2, Special Collections, Baker Library, Harvard Business School; Royal E. Robbins, "Treasurer's Report, 1891, American (Waltham) Watch Company," Annual Report to Shareholders (Waltham Watch Company, 1891), Vol. AD-2, Special Collections, Baker Library, Harvard Business School. Waltham Treasurer's reports 1876-1899.

[498] "Commercial Relations of the United States with Foreign Countries during the Year 1899 Vol II," United States Department of State (Washington, D.C.: Government Printing Office, 1900), 725–26, https://hdl.handle.net/2027/mdp.39015067319833; Using Swiss sources Donzé, *History of the Swiss Watch Industry*, 58 notes that America was the seventh largest market for the Swiss 1901-1910. Author's calculations.

[499] "Commercial Relations of the United States with Foreign Countries during the Year 1899 Vol II," 725–26. Author's calculations.

[500] Royal E. Robbins, "Treasurer's Report, 1882, American (Waltham) Watch Company," Annual Report to Shareholders (Waltham Watch Company, 1882), Vol. AD-2, Special Collections, Baker Library, Harvard Business School for inflation calculations, profit figures have been adjusted to 1860 dollars.

[501] Author's calculations based on data from Waltham's Annual Reports to Shareholders.

[502] Royal E. Robbins, "Treasurer's Report, 1873, American (Waltham) Watch Company," Annual Report to Shareholders (Waltham Watch Company, 1873), Vol. AD-1, Special Collections, Baker Library, Harvard Business School; Robbins, "Treasurer's Report, 1882, American (Waltham) Watch Company."

[503] Moore, *Timing a Century: History of the Waltham Watch Company*, 76.

[504] Tom McIntyre, "Ezra C. Fitch – Watchmaker, Salesman, Inventor, Businessman," (Digital (PDF)), accessed January 15, 2018, http://mcintyre.com/present/ECFitch.pdf.

[505] Moore, *Timing a Century: History of the Waltham Watch Company*, 76.

[506] Moore, 156.

[507] Chandler, *The Visible Hand*, 247 notes that pricing and investment decisions in production companies were often driven by a company's selling agent. Therefore, placing Fitch in the production management role would have struck few as odd.

[508] See Moore, *Timing a Century: History of the Waltham Watch Company*, chap. Appendix B.

[509] Moore, 76.

[510] Moore, 270, Appendix A.

[511] Moore, 270.

[512] Moore, *Timing a Century: History of the Waltham Watch Company*, 270, 91–92 Moore is not clear as to how much authority Robbins maintained. His accounts conflict, at one point calling Robbins' control nominal, at another saying he had unqualified control to exercise his authority.

[513] Chandler, *The Visible Hand*, 146.

[514] Chandler, 145.

[515] Chandler, 146.

[516] Analysis based on Chandler, 145–46 and his observations of development in the railroads.

[517] Moore, *Timing a Century: History of the Waltham Watch Company*, 70.

[518] It was Fitch who pushed to increase Waltham's variety of offerings and models. See Moore, 79, 156.

[519] Robbins, "Treasurer's Report, 1883, American (Waltham) Watch Company," 4.

[520] Moore, *Timing a Century: Histor*

[521] Moore, *Timing a Century: History*

[522] Moore, *Timing a Century: History o)*

[523] Moore, *Timing a Century: History of the*

[524] Moore, 237.

[525] Moore, 175.

[526] Moore, 237.

[527] Moore, 76.

[528] Moore, 76.

[529] Clawson, *Bureaucracy and the Labor Process: The Transfor. Industry 1860-1920*, 240–43.

[530] George W. Blow, "Standard Production Times: Their Need, Determination, and Use in the Waltham Watch Company" (Harv. Business School, 1921), 3, Baker Library Special Collections, Harvar. Business School.

[531] Blow, 5.

[532] David, *American and Swiss Watchmaking in 1876*, 22.

[533] Moore, *Timing a Century: History of the Waltham Watch Company*, 79.

[534] Dennis Yao, "A Note on Anti-Trust and Competitive Tactics (9-703-493)," Course Note (Boston: Harvard Business School Publishing, 2011), 8.

[535] Note: Donze's stats cite Swiss government reports, which show significantly more exports than American government estimates. I have relied on the Swiss data used by Donze as it is probably more accurate. See Donzé, *History of the Swiss Watch Industry*, fig. 2 (p 56).

[536] Favre-Perret, "Philadelphia Exhibition 1876: Presented to the Federal High Council on the Horology Industry," 11.

[537] Landes, "Watchmaking: A Case Study in Enterprise and Change," 12.

[538] Walker, "International Exhibition 1876 Reports and Awards Group XXI," 123.

[539] Walker, 128.

[540] "The American Waltham Watches," *The Allentown Democrat*, February 13, 1884.

[541] "The Waltham Watch," *The Philadelphia Inquirer*, January 31, 1880.

[542] "Cheap and Good Watches," *Lancaster Daily Intelligencer*, April 15, 1880.

[543] "Waltham Watches," *The Boston Globe*, November 9, 1890, 24.

[544] "Gold Watches," *The Boston Globe*, November 12, 1891, 6.

[545] "The Patek, Philippe, and Co Watch," *The Times Herald*, August 15, 1891.

[546] "Patek Philippe & Co," *The Baltimore Sun*, March 20, 1886, 1.

hilippe & Co.s Chronographs!," *The Record-Union*, November 5,

kegren Watch," *The Times*, October 28, 1889, 3.

Ekegren Watch," *Dollar Weekly News*, May 28, 1887, 3.

luable Christmas Gifts," *The Times*, November 28, 1888, 3.

d DeLong, "Economic Distribution--within the United States,"
onal website of Professor Brad DeLong (Berkeley), The U.S. Economy
ck on Top?:" Economic Growth and the Rhetoric of National Power,
ovember 10, 1997, http://www.j-bradford-
elong.net/Econ_Articles/back_on_top.html.

552 Pamela Walker Laird, *Advertising Progress: American Business and the Rise of Consumer Marketing* (Baltimore: Johns Hopkins University Press, 1998), 120.

553 Thorstein Veblen, *The Theory of the Leisure Class: An Economic Study of Institutions [1899]* (New York: Macmillan Company, 1926), 167.

554 Veblen, *The Theory of the Leisure Class: An Economic Study of Institutions [1899]*, 73.

555 Veblen, 74.

556 O'Malley, *Keeping Watch: A History of American Time*, 175.

557 O'Malley, 176.

558 Veblen, *The Theory of the Leisure Class: An Economic Study of Institutions [1899]*, 167–68.

559 "Swiss Watches," *The Watertown News*, March 12, 1884, 3.

560 Author's tabulations based on reported information in "Time O' Day: How a Number of Citizens of Brooklyn Find Out," *The Brooklyn Daily Eagle*, May 14, 1892, 2.

561 Landes, *Revolution in Time*, 325.

562 "Commercial Relations of the United States with Foreign Countries during the Year 1899 Vol II," 723. Luxury Swiss watches by value, as defined by gold-cased or mechanically complicated watches.

563 "Commercial Relations of the United States with Foreign Countries during the Year 1899 Vol II," 723-726. Luxury Swiss watches by value, as defined by gold-cased or mechanically complicated watches.

564 The only well-adjusted luxury watches produced in 1899 were 230 Riverside Maximus watches. Total production data taken from Waltham's 1899 Annual Report. See Tom McIntyre, "Waltham Serial Numbers Database," National Association of Watch and Clock Collectors, accessed January 19, 2018, http://nawccinfo.nawcc.org/LookupSN.php for luxury production data.

565 "Commercial Relations of the United States with Foreign Countries during the Year 1899 Vol II," 725–26 author's calculations.

[566] Swiss data based on "Commercial Relations between U.S. and Switzerland 1899," p. 725-726. Luxury Swiss watches defined as those with complicated movements or a gold case.

[567] New York Mail and Express, "American Watches," *The Atchison Champion*, March 13, 1890, 7.

[568] Moore, *Timing a Century: History of the Waltham Watch Company*, 214.

[569] Using gold watches as a measure of luxury. See Donzé, *History of the Swiss Watch Industry*, 57.

[570] McIntyre, "Waltham Serial Numbers Database"; Roy Ehrhardt, *American Pocket Watch Identification and Price Guide (Book 2)* (Kansas City, MO: Heart of America Press, 1974). Based on the author's calculations.

[571] Royal E. Robbins, "Treasurer's Report, 1884, American (Waltham) Watch Company," Annual Report to Shareholders (Waltham Watch Company, 1884), 4–5, Vol. AD-2, Special Collections, Baker Library, Harvard Business School.

[572] Glasmeier, *Manufacturing Time*, 141.

[573] Thank you to Jon Weber for his contributions and discussions with the author on the value of Swiss modularity on the development of the wristwatch.

[574] Langlois, "Schumpeter and Personal Capitalism Economics Working Paper," 21–22.

[575] Moore, *Timing a Century: History of the Waltham Watch Company*, 165.

[576] Glasmeier, *Manufacturing Time*, 141–43.

[577] Donzé, *History of the Swiss Watch Industry*, 58.

[578] Royal E. Robbins, "Treasurer's Report, American (Waltham) Watch Company" (Waltham Watch Company Records, 1887), 4–6, Vol. AD-2, Baker Library, Harvard Business School.

[579] Return on Assets = total profits / assets. Because Waltham held almost no debt, it is effectively a Return on Equity (ROE) as well. Additionally, because most of Waltham's assets were Operating Assets, it is very close to a Return on Operating Assets (ROA).

[580] Hagel et al.

[581] Hagel et al.

[582] Moore, *Timing a Century: History of the Waltham Watch Company*, 78–79.

[583] Nahum H. Lewis, "Horology of the World's Columbian Exposition, Chicago, 1893, Part 10," *National Association of Watch and Clock Collectors' Bulletin*, December 1987, 465.

[584] Lewis, 381.

[585] *Report of the Committee on Awards of the World's Columbian Commission: Special Reports upon Special Subjects or Groups (Vol II)*, vol. II (Washington

DC: Government Printing Office, 1901), 895,
http://hdl.handle.net/2027/uva.x030527512.

[586] *Report of the Committee on Awards of the World's Columbian Commission*, II:896.

[587] *Report of the Committee on Awards of the World's Columbian Commission*, II:896.

[588] *Report of the Committee on Awards of the World's Columbian Commission*, II:895.

[589] *Report of the Committee on Awards of the World's Columbian Commission*, II:895.

[590] Donzé, "The Creation of Schools of Watchmaking."

[591] *Report of the Committee on Awards of the World's Columbian Commission*, II:896.

[592] *Report of the Committee on Awards of the World's Columbian Commission*, II:895.

[593] *Report of the Committee on Awards of the World's Columbian Commission*, II:896.

[594] Royal E. Robbins, "Treasurer's Report, American (Waltham) Watch Company" (Waltham Watch Company Records, 1894), 3, Vol. AD-2, Baker Library, Harvard Business School; *Report of the Committee on Awards of the World's Columbian Commission*, II:886–87; Converted using Williamson, "Seven Ways to Compute the Relative Value of a U.S. Dollar Amount, 1774 to Present."

[595] "Report of the Committee on Awards of the Columbian Commission (Vol II)," n.d., 886–87.

[596] Nahum H. Lewis, "Horology of the World's Columbian Exposition, Chicago, 1893, Part 3," *National Association of Watch and Clock Collectors' Bulletin*, 1985, 737.

[597] "American Watches: The Exhibit of Domestic Manufacturers at the World's Fair," *New York Tribune*, August 28, 1893, 2.

[598] Robbins, "Treasurer's Report, American (Waltham) Watch Company," 1894, 3.

[599] "Profit Versus Quality (Advertisement)," *Buffalo Morning Express and Illustrated Buffalo Express*, April 18, 1907.

[600] Robbins, "Treasurer's Report, 1878, American (Waltham) Watch Company," 8.

[601] Robbins, "Treasurer's Report, 1879, American (Waltham) Watch Company," 2.

[602] Robbins, "Treasurer's Report, 1882, American (Waltham) Watch Company," 4.

[603] Brenner and Crescenzi, "State Sponsored Crime: The Futility of the Economics Espionage Act," 397.

[604] Donzé, *History of the Swiss Watch Industry*, 66.

[605] David, *American and Swiss Watchmaking in 1876*, sec. Translators' preface.

[606] Barrelet and Bédat, *Preface to the Rapport à la Société intercantonale des industries du Jura sur la fabrication de l'horlogerie aux Etats-Unis, 1876 [Translation of Preface unpublished]*.

[607] Chandler, 8.

[608] Blow, "Standard Production Times: Their Need, Determination, and Use in the Waltham Watch Company," I–9.

[609] Donald Sull, "Why Good Companies Go Bad," *Harvard Business Review*, July 1, 1999, https://hbr.org/1999/07/why-good-companies-go-bad; Chandler would also discuss that competition for profits was usually enough to force the organization to overcome "bureaucratic inertia," but this was evidently not the case at Waltham. See Chandler, *Scale and Scope: The Dynamics of Industrial Capitalism*, 230.

[610] Orin Hatch, "Report 104-359: The Industrial Espionage Act of 1996" (United States Senate, August 27, 1996), 6, https://www.congress.gov/104/crpt/srpt359/CRPT-104srpt359.pdf.

[611] Albrecht Glitz and Erik Meyersson, "Industrial Espionage and Productivity (Working Paper No. 6525)," *CESifo Working Papers*, June 2017, 3.

[612] Hatch, "Report 104-359: The Industrial Espionage Act of 1996," 6.

[613] Moore, 271–72.

[614] John Sherman, "The Sherman Antitrust Act" (1890).

[615] Charles Hulburd, "Letter to Mr. T. Zurbrugg, Pres., Philadelphia Watch Case Company. [The Letters to and from Ezra Fitch, 1904 to 1906]," Typed, March 30, 1905, 1, Box P-1, Folder 1, Baker Library Special Collections, Harvard Business School. Additionally, see Hulburd's letter to Fitch dated April 03, 1905.

Made in the USA
Las Vegas, NV
20 December 2022